LIVING CHRISTIANITY

Martin Palmer, a lay Anglican theologian is head of the multi-faith International Consultancy on Religion, Education and Culture (ICOREC). He has written extensively on religious issues, both from the perspective of a Christian and as someone deeply involved in social, political and inter-religious issues. He is religious adviser to World Wide Fund for Nature (WWF) International and to HRH Prince Philip. A controversial figure, he has frequently been attacked by right-wing and fundamentalist Christians for his work with ecology and with other faiths. He has worked with churches in more than thirty countries and from this practical experience much of his own thinking has arisen. Working daily with people of many faiths, his own faith has been profoundly influenced by these encounters, but it is without hesitation that he describes himself as a Christian – albeit a somewhat unconventional one!

Living Christianity

MARTIN PALMER

ELEMENT

Shaftesbury, Dorset ● Rockport, Massachusetts
Brisbane, Queensland

Published in Great Britain in 1993 by
Element Books Limited
Longmead, Shaftesbury, Dorset

Published in the USA in 1993 by
Element Inc
42 Broadway, Rockport, MA 01966

Published in Australia in 1993 by
Element Books Limited for
Jacaranda Wiley Limited
33 Park Road, Milton, Brisbane 4064

Cover photograph: 'Moods' from the Photo Library International, Leeds
Cover design by Max Fairbrother
Designed by Roger Lightfoot
Map by Taurus Graphics, Kidlington
Typeset by Poole Typesetting (Wessex) Ltd
Printed and bound in Great Britain by
Dotesios Ltd, Trowbridge, Wiltshire

British Library Cataloguing in Publication
data available

Library of Congress Cataloging in Publication
data available

ISBN 1–85230–327–1

Contents

Acknowledgements

The version of the creed, reproduced on pp. 72–4, by Jay Ramsay, 1992, is dedicated to the memory of his grandfather, the Revd. George Edward Brown (1876–1941) in memory of his sacrifice.

This book is dedicated with love to Derek Palmer, father, priest and friend. It is offered as a thanksgiving for all the saints whose names are now no longer known except to God, but who kept the candle of faith alive down the ages.

1

Why Bother with Christianity?

As a child growing up in the early sixties in Bristol, my understanding of Christianity was predominantly shaped by two very different churches. On the working-class housing estate where we lived, our church was a humble affair built in the late fifties. There was nothing special about it architecturally. It had no history, no interesting monuments or ancient arches. But it was the centre of a community of ordinary people whose lives were shaped, enriched, comforted, celebrated and mourned within its walls, in its community hall and in its area. Here, Sunday after Sunday, a small but faithful group gathered. Here, those who had no other place to turn to when in trouble came and knew they would be accepted. Here the families of the estate – working-class Bristolians resettled on the outskirts of their war-battered city – made new lives for themselves. In the parish church of St Andrew's they came to give thanks for births, to celebrate marriages and to mourn those who had died. We Christians were in a minority and without any real power. The church was often robbed, vandalized and scorned. Yet it kept going through the energies of the faithful and because the community wanted the church to 'be there'.

The second church spoke of a different world and told a different story. Fifteen miles away from my housing estate, across the gaunt and beautiful Mendip hills, lies the ancient cathedral city of Wells. Here the entire city (with a population roughly the same size as the housing estate – 20,000 people) is dominated by the massive and wonderful cathedral. When life on the tough, ugly housing estate got too much for me, I would set off across the hills to Wells, on foot, by bus or on my bicycle. In Wells I found a world where the Church was the power in the land. A world of history and magnificent architecture; of the tombs of bishops who had been the chancellors of England, and who had made and broken kings; of treasures given by the wealthy and the powerful, and monuments recording those who saw themselves as the great and the good. In my fifteen-mile journey I had left the arena of the Christian faith in a largely secular, impoverished, post-Christian world and walked into the world of the power, authority and magnificence of Christendom.

As a child I was fascinated by these two Christian models; I found much within both which attracted me and which I could see spoke with purpose and intensity to the different worlds they inhabited. I was proud of the small but lively community of Christians to which I belonged on the housing estate. I was moved by the compassion, care and effort which they put into building up the wider community in which we lived. In the lives of railway engineers, cleaning ladies, plumbers and secretaries for whom being a Christian carried no power, status or privileges, it was possible to feel a link with the first Christians. Here were people for whom faith was costly; people who were mocked for bothering to believe at all. I saw manifested the fellowship of the disciples and the love and suffering of Christ. In the rebuilding, time and time again, of the youth centre, vandalized on average every three months, the experience of the crucifixion and resurrection was acted out time and again, as people who gave their time and money saw it go to waste, but began again.

In walking to Wells I sought testimony that Christianity had once been more powerful. I was moved by the beauty which faith can inspire. By the authority that faith can exercise. Then one wintry evening I walked into the cathedral as they sang evensong. I was transported to a different plane. Footsore and tired, I was refreshed and restored in a way which I cannot adequately describe. This was the point at which I realized that

Christianity is not just about fellowship here on earth but is about the transcendent and the breaking in of the eternal and infinite into our world – whatever world that might be.

From these two different churches and their different stories and communities and worlds, I have been able to continue to explore the diversity and variety of ways in which this strange faith expresses itself and moves and is moved by the cultures in which it lives. This has been done, not with any anthropological interest, but simply because for better or for worse I have continued to grapple with what Christianity means to me and to my world.

THE STORIES OF CHRISTIANITY

The purpose of this book is relatively straightforward. Too many of us have only encountered one or perhaps two of the worlds of Christianity. In many cases, what we have encountered has seemed archaic or irrelevent. The faith doesn't seem to speak to our world, or if it does, it speaks of a world now largely gone. Thus many of my generation have rejected Christianity having heard just one of its stories or explanations of its meaning and purpose. In the USA, this tends to be the shrill story of the tele-evangelists; in England it is the confused voices of the Anglican Church wondering about the status of women. In the light of contemporary social concerns, the past influence of the Church is seen to have fed the growth of capitalism and the rise of sexism, and to have indoctrinated us with a view of human superiority which has led us to abuse the planet. Its current attempts to be relevant are often seen as jumping on the bandwagon as it passes by.

Yet for millions around the world, Christianity tells a story which helps them oppose the life-denying forces which others see as having their historical roots in Western Christianity. Others are taking key elements of the faith and fashioning new understandings and models by which they seek to live and to assist their societies in understanding the world around them. And throughout the last 2000 years there have been undercurrents, local churches and entire branches of the faith which have pursued radically different paths from that of its dominant political and social forms.

This book looks at the different major stories of the faith and how some of these stories, long buried and almost forgotten, have power and truth for us today. We cannot go back to these stories and try to adopt them for the worlds from which they arose have largely disappeared. However, we can see that they were faithful to their time and culture and spoke through and within them in a way which can illustrate how we need to rediscover that it is both right and possible to tell our own version of Christianity.

So why bother with Christianity, with these stories? As someone who works in inter-faith work and on environmental issues, I am often asked why I still remain a Christian. At one level my answer is very simple. It still makes more sense of the world than any other system I have encountered. But I also still believe because I see myself as part of the process of retelling the story of Christ and the meaning of the incarnation – a retelling which millions of others are engaged in, consciously and subconsciously.

I am often driven to exasperation and deep anger by much of what is said and done – and not said and done – in the name of my faith. I despair of many Christian structures, from the doddering Church of England to the so-called radical World Council of Churches, but I am rarely disappointed at the stories individual Christians have to tell of their struggle to be faithful to their faith and to the world in which God has placed them. This book is an attempt to legitimize the right to tell our stories of the faith and to encourage others to begin to explore the story they have to tell and how the stories of Christianity might touch and enlighten their own narrative.

As this book is about stories, let me start with two – stories which seem to speak of very different kinds of Christianity, and of their ability to speak of their Lord to this world.

The Saint and the Plastic

My son and I had decided that during the Easter holidays we would follow in the footsteps of some of the great Celtic saints of Britain. Our travels took us up into Scotland and in particular to the lowland areas around Galloway. Here, in the late fourth century, the first recorded stone church in Britain was built. Its founder was the hermit monk Ninian. Ninian was a Briton, which means he was almost certainly a Celt. His father and grandfather had been priests of Christ and Ninian was obviously destined for this path. Ninian travelled to Rome and possibly to the Holy Land. On his way back he visited a remarkable experiment which was just beginning in Gaul. St Martin had founded the first monastery there – almost certainly the first in the Western Church. Here Ninian saw a new and exciting model of Christian life in the midst of a collapsing and corrupt society.

Inspired by this vision, Ninian returned to his native land and founded the first monastic community in Britain. The site of his stone-built church—Candida Casa in Latin, meaning the white house, is now the town of Whithorn.

My son and I visited all the sites we could find to do with Ninian, his island, the ruins of his church and the site of his community. Finally we journeyed to a remote part of Galloway to visit his cave. We had read how Ninian would come to this seashore cave to meditate and pray. Here we felt, we could come close to the great saint. Here we could feel him communing with nature – an aspect of Celtic Christianity which we were especially keen to encounter.

So, full of hope, we set off down a little track, trodden by over 1500 years of pilgrims' feet. Our path took us towards the sea through a beautiful tree-lined narrow valley. Alongside us ran a little stream, bright and clear and edged with flowers and sheep-cropped grass. It seemed as if for a moment we had travelled back in time.

The little river disgorges itself on to the beach, and disappears into the pebbles. But before we reached the narrow mouth of the valley we could hear a strange sound, like the rustling of paper or the flapping of shrouds. In that holy place, it was rather odd, if not a little uncanny, not least because we could not work out what was causing it.

As we rounded the last corner, the cause became all too apparent. The mouth of the valley was lined with small, wind-stunted bushes. From every one of these hung plastic; plastic bags, plastic sheets, plastic streamers. In horror we looked about for the source of all this rubbish. No house could be seen. Before us was only the Irish Sea; no sign, bar this plastic effluent, that human beings existed on the planet. As we watched, yet another piece of plastic billowed in from the sea, refuse thrown overboard from some passing ship or carried on the tide from some pleasure beach or town refuse dump miles away.

We picked our way through the tattered shrouds of plastic and made our way to the little cave of St Ninian. From the cave it was almost impossible to see or hear the rubbish. But we knew it was there, and that this sight was one which Ninian, and pilgrims after him for all the centuries until our own, would never have encountered.

This experience shook me. It shook me for a number of reasons and raised questions about the relevance of such an ancient faith as Christianity when faced with the harsh realities of contemporary life and its by-products. Was I guilty of romanticism in seeking in the company of a Celtic saint a world which has virtually gone for ever? Could there be anything from so long ago that could speak to our condition today? If there was, then where were the exciting experiments and new models of community which could be the way forward for our times, in the way that St Martin and St Ninian provided a new model at the time of the collapse of the Western Roman Empire?

I will explore some of these issues more deeply later in this chapter. But now let me move on to my second story.

The Army and the Monastery

It was a cold, grey day in St Petersburg. In an elegant but decaying suburb of the city was the home and office of the Russian Orthodox bishop. Here I and a colleague working with the World Wide Fund for Nature (WWF) International, had come to meet the bishop, Metropolitan John. Our purpose was to discuss ways in which WWF and other environmental groups could work with the Church in Russia, and in particular in the area of St Petersburg, on environmental issues.

We sat in the beautiful old dining room of the metropolitan; at one end of the room were a mass of ancient icons. Here the bishop told us of the terrible state of the environment generally in Russia; of the dying lakes, polluted rivers, foul estuaries and disappearing forests. He was very depressed by all that had happened there. We then asked him what the major environmental problems facing his Church were, especially with regard to the many monasteries and their associated lands which the State was handing back to the Church. His answer gave us a considerable shock.

'Our biggest problem,' he said 'is the number of our monasteries which are radioactive.'

At first I could not believe my ears and asked my colleague who was translating to ask him what he meant. There was no mistake. The bishop was telling us that some fifteen monasteries in his diocese were radioactive. The next question from us was, how?

The explanation was simple. The monasteries had been seized from the Church after the 1917 Revolution and because of their size and form, they had proved ideal as barracks for the army. In some of these monastery barracks, nuclear weapons were stored and sometimes dismantled. In certain cases, nuclear waste was buried on the sites. The net result of this is a series of radioactive monasteries which the Church has been given back in the hope that in some way, it could repair the terrible damage done. Indeed, this seems to be the reason for giving back most of the seized Church land and buildings. The land is exhausted and the buildings – with a few notable exceptions – (in a terrible state. The State hopes that the Church will be able to bring back to life what the State has killed or deeply wounded.

What a strange contrast to my experience in Scotland. With St Ninian's cave, the invasion of the pollution of modern life and its philosophies seemed a comment on the apparent irrelevance of what St Ninian stood for. In a society such as Britain, where the Church as an institution is largely ignored or marginalized, what earthly significance could the faith held by Ninian have to the practical problems of today? Meanwhile, in Russia, where the Government has created massive disasters, it is to the Church that it turns for a way forward into the next millennium, for a liveable alternative to the now defunct and discredited secularism and Marxism of the Communist State. And it is to the Church that people are coming in such vast numbers that the authorities have given up trying to count the number of new converts.

Now I happen to believe that there is in fact a great deal in common between these stories, for I believe that the faith of Ninian and the experience of the Russian Orthodox Church alike offer us models for the way forward. But for the moment I want to use the two stories to look at how the Christian faith is seen so very differently in the two cultures: the cultures of the West, namely North America, much of Western Europe and Australia/New Zealand – the rich third of the world; and the cultures of the poorer two-thirds – the former Soviet Union, Eastern Europe, Africa, Asia and Latin America.

THE DYING CHURCH

To many in the West, the Church is irrelevant. Fewer and fewer people attend church, though the pattern varies enormously. The USA has a high attendance figure with over 40 per cent of adults in church every Sunday. In Scandinavia, the figure is around 3–4 per cent. The UK is perhaps a fair indicator of the middle ground. All the mainstream churches have been losing members over the last ten years. The figures differ in the different regions, but in the country as a whole, 15 per cent of the adult population are regular church goers. The denominations which during the eighties lost most members were the Roman Catholics (17 per cent), the Anglicans (15 per cent), the Presbyterian/United Reform Church (14 per cent), and the Methodists (11 per cent). But at the same time two denominations experienced a growth. The most dramatic was the independent churches whose membership rose by 67 per cent. The Orthodox churches which were small to begin with, nevertheless had a growth rate of 27 per cent. So while the historical churches of the UK are in decline, the newer ones (in the British context) are growing.

A similar pattern can be found in most countries in what I have termed the West. In the USA, the crisis is even more pronounced. The growth of independent churches, fundamentalist sects and TV ministries has greatly weakened the older mainstream churches, with the exception of the Southern Baptists. All the mainstream churches are cutting back on their staff and programmes owing to the major shortfalls in giving resulting from the decline in numbers. Meanwhile, despite setbacks such as the 'sexcapades' of some TV evangelists, the right-wing, fundamentalist or independent churches continue to grow – especially amongst the marginalized groups such as the Hispanics. One of the major features of such churches, both in the USA and in Europe, is their support of the status quo. Thus there is little interest in tackling social and economic issues such as the environment, social welfare or development issues. The core of the gospel for such groups is to save people from the fires of damnation.

Also within this area of growth are those who believe that the end of time, Armageddon, is just around the corner. Using bits of texts from the Bible, they almost seem to gloat with glee at signs of economic and environmental collapse. During the Gulf War of 1991, many such groups predicted that this was the trigger which would launch the Third World War and bring the Antichrist to power, thus making it possibe for Christ to return at the head of a heavenly army. Given that such Christians believe that when Jesus returns he will bring in an age of total bliss for the faithful, you can see why they would welcome signs of the End of Days.

Looking at contemporary Christianity in the West, the outsider could be forgiven for feeling what I felt suddenly at the mouth of the valley of St Ninian. What relevance does this faith have to today's issues and today's world? The faithful are diminishing overall, and those groups which are increasing would on the whole not see social issues such as pollution as being important, and would dismiss them as being issues with which the Church should not become involved.

The outside observer could also be forgiven for feeling that not only is Christianity today largely irrelevant to the majority of people, but it is to some degree directly to blame for the mess we are in. Taking the environment and economics as two areas, many would claim that Christianity has either actually created the conditions we now live in, or at the very least, has done little to protest against them. Critics have pointed to the command to Adam to dominate the world:

> And God blessed them and said to them: 'Be fruitful and multiply and fill the earth and subdue it and have dominion over the fish of the sea and over the fowl of the air, and over every living thing that moves upon the earth. (Genesis 1:28)

This mandate is of course capable of two interpretations: stewardship and mastery. The stewardship interpretation says we should be careful of what we use. We have the power of life and death, but we must exercise it with discretion and use nature wisely, not exploit it. The mastery interpretation says we can do what we like. Both leave the rest of creation out of the equation except in terms of their usefulness to humanity. Here, critics say, is where the human-centred model of the world comes from. Here are the seeds of our exploitative and rapacious relationship with everything else God created.

In the arena of economics, Christianity stands condemned by many for having unleashed usury and capitalism upon the world. The links between Protestantism and capitalism have been well explored by such writers as Tawney, while John

Calvin is often cited by alternative economists as being the first theologian to sanction interest and usury. From the Protestant work ethic and the capitalist/interest banking system supported by Protestant theologians has sprung the world economic system which many see as bringing increased poverty and degradation to the vast majority of the world's population.

These are heavy charges, and not all their attacks are actually valid. However, enough remains that is true for those of us who are Christians to feel uncomfortable and to have to look long and hard at the darker side of our faith. Given such a history, many in the West would argue, what can Christianity possibly offer to a world choking on its own plastic rubbish, thrown away by the consumerist, capitalist society? Instead of being surprised and offended to find plastic marring the way to the hermit's cave, such critics would claim that such a sight is the logical result of the processes which Christianity has unleashed upon our world.

Some would say that any expectation that Christianity, the faith which illuminated the path of St Martin, St Ninian and so many others in history, can be relevant today is pure romanticism, the sort of romantic nostalgia with which I and my son strolled down the sylvan path by the bubbling brook to pay homage at the saint's cave. It may be fine to think about on summery afternoons in the shade of ancient church walls or looking out over untouched countryside. It may be well to recite moving prayers about the wind and rain, but ultimately, isn't it all a retreat from the glare of car headlights, the smell of spilt oil, the run-down city centres and the destruction of lives in armed warfare?

To some degree there is truth in this charge. Much of the way Christianity is taught to us is unrealistic and unrelated to real life. This means that many children, as they grow up, reject this milkpap Christianity when they graduate from primary to secondary school. Just as they leave Father Christmas behind, so they leave nostalgic Christianity behind, except for those periods of the year when society allows a wallowing in nostalgia and religion – Christmas being perhaps the prime example of this.

The fact is that many of our contemporaries find Christianity quaint, good for holiday visits and nicely warming when old hymns or carols are sung at special times. But as for it being the very medium through which to interpret and understand their everyday life – forget it!

However, there are some Christians who present what might be described as a more robust response to the issues of the present day. Not for them the nostalgia, the harking back to a golden time when the faith walked tall amongst the green fields and faithful hamlets. For these Christians the world today can be read and interpreted as a divine plan working up to its denouement. For them the wars, rumours of wars, civil strife and rivalry between power blocks are all signs of the end of time. They believe that Christ will come in power and glory when we have so bowed ourselves to the forces of the Antichrist that the world itself is in a state of constant warfare and massive environmental pollution. They see all this foretold in the books of Daniel and Revelation in the Bible. For them, the disasters of the world are foretold and inevitable. To try and fight against them is to play into the hands of the devil.

The ability of such Christians to find texts in the Bible for all key developments in society today is quite remarkable. The creation of the state of Israel is a primary issue for them (Ezekiel 36: 24); the European Community is one of the necessary beasts which must arise to be overthrown by Christ (Daniel 7: 7–8); the United Nations, the World Council of Churches and plastic credit cards and microchip technology are all apparently foretold in Revelation 13. As for AIDS, this is just the start of the scourges God will send upon earth (Job 36: 14), along with the necessary destruction of the planet's natural resources (Revelation 8: 7–11). Many within the secular world hear the rantings of such Biblical prophecy Christians and have their sense that Christianity is irrelevant even more forcefully confirmed.

Nor do the mainstream churches fare much better. As an Anglican I have had to watch my church waste twenty years on internecine warfare over the ordination of women. In a society where the equality of women is at least on the statute books and where most organizations have made some effort to incorporate it into their practices, the Church has stood out like a sore thumb. By a mixture of naïvety, misogyny, uncertainty and God knows what other problems, a simple issue – can women be ordained to the priesthood – has tied up resources and energies in a way considered frankly farcical by most people outside. No doubt in thirty or more years' time we shall all look back at this and shake our heads in wonder that such a straightforward move should have taken so long and have been gained at such cost. But at the moment, it is still absorbing the life spirit of so much of the Church and making it an object of ridicule. As a believer, this saddens me.

These are but some of the reflections about the oft-perceived role of Christianity in the West! dwindling, historically compromised, nostalgic and occasionally nutty, but ultimately irrelevant.

THE LIVING CHURCH

Move out of the West and the story is radically different. Far from dwindling or being irrelevant, Christianity is seen as one of the great forces of society helping to map out the future. Take the story of the Bishop of St Petersburg and his radioactive monasteries. Having experimented with the most massive social engineering scheme in history, the Russians have discovered that it has failed. The cost of this failure to the land and environment is only exceeded by the cost to Russia's people. From this mess and failure of ideology the people, and in increasing measure the State, have turned to the only body which consistently bore witness to an alternative model of reality – the Church. In Russia, the Church is growing at such a pace that all its institutions are strained to bursting point. In part, the growth is a response to the lifting of suppression, in part to a flight from the harsh realities of a collapsing world. But within all this there is much genuine and profound searching for a new way forward for the people, based upon values which have served them well in the past. There is little space for nostalgia in a Church which has to deal with radioactive monasteries, entire modern cities – the so-called scientific cities –

without a single church building, and which is having to train from scratch specialist workers in all spheres of life. A Church which is being asked to send chaplains into the notorious psychiatric hospitals, for so long the centres of terrible abuse of people's minds, has few illusions about the world it inhabits or the depths to which human beings can sink.

Nor is Russia an isolated example. In terms of world growth, Christianity so often seen as the faith of the colonialists and Western exploiters, is now massively a poor-world faith. The vast majority of Christians live in Africa, Asia and Latin America. In Africa it is estimated that there are 16,000 new converts to Christianity a day (a figure quoted by the Ecumenical Documentation and Information Centre of Eastern and Southern Africa).

In many countries, the Christian faith is a vital and vibrant factor in both personal and social life. Take Kenya, for instance. Here the churches have been the only continuing organization through which dissent has been possible under the one-party system. Every day the newspapers carry extensive reports on the sayings and actions of church leaders. As for the Monday papers, I have never seen such extensive reporting of sermons! It is taken for granted that what some church leader finds sufficiently important to preach about is of significance to the nation.

Kenya is far from unique; and even in the former Communist bloc, the actions and sayings of the Church are deemed to be of importance to the thinking and active life of the people. In many countries, the *de facto* opposition of the churches means that they are news. From the fading juntas of Latin America to the civil wars of Sri Lanka and South Africa via the revolutions of Poland and Haiti, the Churches have played a key role in the struggle for justice, for new models of government and for the democratic rights of the people.

THE CHRISTIAN INFLUENCE ON THE WEST

There seems therefore to be a vast difference in the influence and significance of Christianity in the West – and in the rest of the world. Yet even in the West, the influence of Christianity is much more powerful and pervasive than might at first be assumed. We are, whether we like it or not, societies formed and forged upon the anvil of Christianity. One example is the growth of a scientific culture. While China and India were able to develop very sophisticated scientific cultures, they never came close to the developments in scientific exploration and discovery which Western culture has achieved.

The main reason for this is that in the West, over the last 600–700 years, Roman Catholic and Protestant Christianity have desanctified nature. Whereas Hinduism and Taoism taught that the One was to be found in the many and the many in the One, Western Christianity taught a very clear divide between God and God's creation. By doing so, it made it both possible and even desirable that human beings should explore and test nature. By making nature separate from the divine, it allowed it to become ordinary, and thus to experiment or use nature was not to attack the divine.

This desanctification of nature meant that the processes of exploration, investigation and hypothesizing which are the hallmarks of contemporary science, were able to develop. It was Christianity which, for better or for worse, enabled this to happen.

Look at the ways in which we frighten ourselves when we feel we are going down a path which is destructive. The peace movement and the environmental movement are both examples of responses to crises which have fallen back on apocalyptic, end-of-the-world type language to get across to the wider public the seriousness of the mess we are in. This is because Western culture works on a biblically dominated model of time. By this I don't mean that we all believe in a six-day creation. That is irrelevant. What we do believe in is that time is linear – it goes from A to Z and does not go round in circles. Thus, whether we call it the first day of creation or the big bang, our scientific and religious models, derived from Christianity, give us a definite start to creation. The corollary of this is that we also believe that time will have a definite end. The classic descriptions of this appear in the books of Daniel and Revelation in the Bible. The imagery used there has passed into common parlance and it is this language, this model of time as having a beginning and an end, which we use in order both to make sense of time and to spur us into action when threats arise to our future.

However, large parts of the world do not believe time is linear. They believe it is cyclical, without a definite beginning or end. There is no evidence which could decide the argument one way or another. We in the West take it for granted that we are right and time is linear. But this is incapable of proof and is an example of the way we uncritically take models of reality from the Bible.

It is these models of reality – time as linear, you only live once, nature is separate from God and so forth – which show the abiding influence and power of Christianity on our culture. We therefore delude ourselves if we think we inhabit a rational, secular society. In fact we inhabit a world which to outsiders is full of myths, ideas they find odd and beliefs which we have inherited, usually uncritically, and which we simply believe to be true. One of the tasks of this book is to look at these myths, beliefs and values and to ask: are they faithful to the heart of Christianity, and, are they of any use to us as we confront the problems and opportunities that are currently arising?

2

Stories from the Journeys of Christianity

When I was a student grappling with being a Christian, I found great difficulty with the world view of the New Testament. I do not believe in devils or evil spirits for instance. I felt that this disqualified me from being a Christian until I heard the great Dr Joseph Needham talking. He is a scientist, a sinologist (his major work is the multi-volume *Science and Civilisation in China*), a Marxist and a devout Anglican. He said quite simply and bluntly that he didn't and couldn't believe in the world of the first century Christians. It simply made no sense to him, given what he knew about the world. However, this did not stop him being a Christian. He said that he was able to comprehend and make sense of his world of the twentieth century through his faith, in just the same way that the first century Christians made sense of their world. That the worlds are completely different did not affect the ability of the faithful to understand them. But it was ridiculous to make people adopt the outlook and mentality of the first century in order to be Christians. That was not what Christianity was about.

This is a very important point. The reason Christianity persists is precisely because it helps us to understand ourselves, our world and God in whatever context we find ourselves. There is nothing less sacred about driving cars than there is about herding sheep. The fact that the Bible uses imagery drawn from the sheep-herding world of northern Palestine does not mean that that is what makes sense to us today.

So I want to explore just some of the stories of Christianity down the ages. I want to take you through a few of the major developments and diverse cultures which interacted with the faith and produced particular manifestations at particular times. We should see the stories as dynamic. Christianity is, and always has been, changing. At times, I shall be arguing, it has made great mistakes, most of which it has then recognized and corrected. At times it has forced out teachings which were truly dangerous, and at other times it has absorbed them. At times it has expelled insights and groups whose witness was crucial to a more wholesome Christianity, at other times it has accepted the challenges such groups or insights have presented to its own self-understanding.

'WHO DO PEOPLE SAY THAT I AM?'

The origin of our stories is the same. The event of the Incarnation, the coming of Jesus Christ, the Word of God made flesh. Most people have no problem with the teachings of Jesus Christ. Indeed, many feel that if it was just his teachings which we were asked to accept, they could do so. But the Christian faith is not just about Jesus' teachings. Christianity does not just say 'Here is a great teacher, follow his teachings.' It says that the person and very being of Jesus Christ, who he was and is, why he came and what he manifested, are as important as his teachings if not more so.

One of the crucial moments in the gospels comes when Jesus asks his disciples, 'Who do people say that I am?' The answers are varied, ranging from John the Baptist come back to life to Elijah or one of the other prophets. Then Peter says 'You are the Christ, the Son of the living God.' (Matthew 16: 13–16)

What this means is what Christianity has been wrestling with ever since. For the Church bears witness to Jesus being not just a man, but also God, not just a great teacher but a witness to God, not just an historical person, but eternal, not just created, but also the creative Word of God.

Furthermore, Christianity has always been a missionary faith.

It has a vision of what should and could be for all humanity. It has teachings about who and what we are that make sense of the worlds we inhabit, both external and internal. It has a powerful sense that these insights or truths are for all people everywhere and thus it seeks to share them. However, from its earliest days Christianity came into contact with forces outside the world of Judaism which profoundly influenced the way it understood itself and its message. This process of interaction has continued ever since and has given us, for better or for worse, the Christianities of the world today and of the past. So let me try and introduce you to the extraordinary stories that are Christianity.

RELIGIOUS PLURALISM, ROMAN STYLE

Christianity did not grow up in isolation in the first century. The era was one of immense religious upheaval. As the Roman Empire consolidated its hold over vast tracts of more ancient civilizations (such as Egypt, Palestine, Syria, parts of Persia and Greece), so it came into contact with a whole host of deities and religions. As the Roman deities were largely civil functionaries elevated to the heavens, the attraction of more vibrant and dramatic religions was obvious. The first century saw a plethora of new religious movements arriving in Rome and growing in the provinces. Many of these were esoteric cults or mystery religions like Mithraism. Here, in secret gatherings, people were initiated into a religious élite. In a world of tremendous cosmopolitanism, identity and meaning were to be found in belonging to a special group with its own symbols and codes of behaviour.

At first, Christianity was simply one amongst many of the new religious movements, rejected by its parent faith Judaism, and not really comfortable in the wider, non-Jewish world of the Gentiles. Its teachings about a god-man were not that unusual – other faiths had similar ideas. Nor was its message about death and resurrection particularly novel – the cult of Osiris from Egypt was a well-known one. What was exciting about Christianity to the Roman world, was the fact that it made it possible to believe in the one God of Judaism without all the ritual and circumcision of Judaism. For many years, Judaism had attracted Gentiles who were intrigued by the belief in just one God, the denial of the validity of other gods and the strong moral and ethical teachings which sprang from such a faith. The translation of the Hebrew Bible into Greek in the third century BC meant that many Gentiles were familiar with its teachings (Greek, not Latin being then the common language of the eastern Mediterranean). However, the strict laws of the Jews prevented all but the most determined from actually converting.

PLATO MEETS MOSES

In the Bible, Gentiles found that the one God idea, which Plato had also put forward, was fused with a mystery and a dynamic which were missing from both Plato's idea of the divine and much of conventional formal religion. Christianity offered as it were the best of the rational philosophical thought, mixed with the spice of the mystery religions. This, combined with a strong sense of both the importance of the individual and the significance of the community and society at large, offered a unique combination. Here was no attempt to appease or negotiate with the gods, capricious as ever. Here was the one God, reaching out in love to humanity. This was in itself a major breakthrough in religious thought for much of the Gentile world.

Within the original band of followers of Jesus, this interest on the part of the Gentiles was a problem. As far as we can tell, all Jesus' disciples were Jewish, though he certainly had followers amongst the Gentiles, such as the centurion whose servant was ill and the Syro-Phoenician woman he met at the well. But these people are not mentioned as part of the inner circle. The names of all the apostles indicate that they were Jews.

At first the early church seemed very unsure about whether to move beyond the borders of Judaism. They still saw Jesus as the Jewish Messiah, sent to the Jews themselves. Had not the Maccabees in the second century BC fought against the attempts of the Greeks to subvert and then actually to wipe out Judaism?

Would it not be the same if they mixed Greek thought with Jewish beliefs?

Into this debate, the first major question about the purpose of Jesus – Jewish Messiah or Messiah of the world – came Saul the pharisee, renamed Paul after his conversion on the road to Damascus. Paul was converted very soon after Jesus' death, but as far as we know had never actually met Jesus. His experience of the living Christ was of the resurrected Christ who spoke to him from the blinding light on the road to Damascus. Paul marked a new step in the development of Christianity, out of the hands of those who knew Jesus in the flesh, to those who encountered him as the risen Lord. Paul also confronted the issue of the contact with the Gentiles. He was adamant. Jesus made all such divisions irrelevant. His message and his purpose was the salvation of all humanity by bringing the message of the kingdom of God.

After hard discussions with Peter, Paul convinced him and the other disciples that the good news was meant for all people and that to become a Christian you did not have to be or become a Jew. This freed the Church from one set of regulations, though there remained a group of Jewish Christians who maintained that you did have to be a Jew to be a Christian. This group was almost totally wiped out when the Jewish rebellion of AD 66–70 was crushed by the Romans, though there are still reports of Jewish Christian groups as late as the beginning of the fourth century. Interestingly, in present-day Christian circles, there have appeared a few small groups who claim that Christians should keep all the dietary and other social laws of the Old Testament. These groups, sometimes known as Israelite Christians follow strict Jewish law. Elements of this approach are also found in groups such as the Jehovah Witnesses. But on the whole, one can say that the purely Jewish understanding of Jesus was the first set of ideas to be sidelined by the Church.

So the Church took on board the Gentiles, and in doing so it began to speak in their language. None of the New Testament is written in Hebrew and only a few words remain of the original language of Jesus, Aramaic (see Mark 5: 41 for instance). As a literary phenomenon, Christianity is a Gentile faith, written in the language of the Greeks and increasingly using their terms of reference. The most famous example of this is the opening of the Gospel of St John. Here, Jesus is described using terminology which arises straight from the philosophical world of the Greeks, but touched with the emotion and power of the Hebrew world. Christianity is already making itself a part of a world and society which lies beyond that of its founder, Jesus, but it does so because it believes that that same Jesus, the Aramaic-speaking Galilean, is also the Lord of all life and of all peoples.

ST PAUL

St Paul is a figure from whom many turn in frustration. For instance, he has been blamed for inculcating sexism into Christianity with his comments about women knowing their place. There is no question that Paul does reflect or even over emphasize the contemporary view of his time that women should be subservient to their husbands and that the only role for women is in the home. It is even possible, as some have claimed, that Paul had a deep dislike if not actual hatred of women. He certainly viewed sex as a necessary evil and in doing so planted a small time-bomb in Christianity. But Paul was also a classic case of someone who took the vision of Christianity as he found it and expanded it to take on board and absorb new world views, which then became part of the world view of Christianity.

The Christianity which Paul so strongly fought for, against those who wished to make it a magical cult, a mystery cult or even an élitist cult, was in fact a pluralist faith. Paul helped Christianity spread by drawing upon Biblical and non-Biblical insights, terms of reference and beliefs. He saw clearly that Christianity, through its belief in the kingdom brought by Jesus, could and did transcend all human barriers. He even went so far as to say that all cultures had borne witness to God before Christ came and that such cultures thus had good within them.

This is not to deny that Paul also loaded the young faith with some pretty undesirable social teachings, which owed more to his views and to the values of his culture than they did to the freedom brought by Jesus Christ. But for him, time was running out. Like all the other first Christians, he expected Jesus to return any day. Thus, while culture was important as a means of reaching the unsaved, it was all going to end any day now. For Paul the kingdom of God was about to appear on earth. The kingdom had formed the central plank of Jesus' teaching. The opening statement of his ministry was, according to Luke, to read from the prophet Isaiah:

> 'The Spirit of the Lord is upon me,
> He has appointed me to preach the good news to the poor,
> to heal the brokenhearted,
> to bring deliverance to the prisoners,
> sight to the blind,
> to free those who are hurt
> and to declare the year of the Lord.'

Closing the book, Jesus said 'Today, this scripture has come true before you.'
(Luke 4: 18–19).

THE COMING OF THE KINGDOM

Mark makes it clear what Jesus understood to be his message. After the account of his baptism by John, Mark says that Jesus came to Galilee preaching the gospel of the kingdom of God and saying, 'The time is fulfilled and the kingdom of God is at hand. Repent and believe in the gospel.'

Jesus seems to have believed that his role was to announce the new order, the kingdom of God which was to come upon earth – exactly as the Lord's prayer requests. The early Christians thought that this meant a physical kingdom. Indeed, one could say that the very first, wrong, interpretation of Christianity or to be more precise, of Jesus, was by Judas Iscariot who thought that Jesus had to come to establish a new Jewish state.

As time went by, it became obvious that Jesus was not about

to return. In Paul's writings one can see this realization dawning. It thus becomes necessary to reinterpret the return of Jesus and indeed to reinterpret the kingdom of God. The return of Jesus is pushed into the future and is given two possible scenarios. The first is that as the Church establishes the kingdom of God on earth through its own existence, the conditions will become right for Jesus to return, for all the world will then acknowledge him. This is what one might call the optimistic future view of Christianity. The second scenario is that when things have got so bad, and evil, violence and apostasy have reached unbearable proportions, then Jesus will return at the head of the avenging angels and all the unjust will get their come-uppance. This is the pessimistic view. Of this school of thought, the Revelation of St John is perhaps the most dramatic example.

These two views of the conditions which human society could or would create which would evoke or provoke the return of Jesus, have surfaced time and time again throughout the history of the Church. We shall meet them as the stories unfold. It is one of the key struggles within the mind of Christianity, and its early origins show how fundamental a split there is between those who view humanity as capable of good and those who see it as essentially bad

The other way of dealing with the crisis of the non-reappearance of Jesus was to take the idea of the kingdom and make it something which had already begun and which was growing like a seed. Thus the notion started that the kingdom was amongst us, if only we could discern it. It saw the conversion of each Christian as a beginning. It saw the mutual respect and corporate life in the Church communities as a sign of this kingdom. It began to see the Church as this kingdom and thus began the road towards the kingdom being identical or synonymous with the Church – a path which was to have major consequences when the Church had control of society.

As the Church began to lose faith in an immediate return of Christ, it had to face the problem which affects all movements which then become institutions: how to order itself and its relationships with the outside world. With the decline in the expectation of the immediate return, came the rise of what one could accurately call the Church as a structure and organization.

Let us be quite clear though that at this stage, around AD 80 Christianity was still a small faith, largely working- or slave-class, with a band of middle-class members and a few aristocratic supporters. The vast majority were now Gentiles and the idea of Christianity being only for the Jews had almost disappeared. The next 200 years saw the consolidation of this trend and the rise of Christianity as a largely socially acceptable but sometimes persecuted faith within the Roman Empire.

Outside the Empire, Christianity was spreading into Ethiopia and Persia. In the Acts of the Apostles we have the story of St Philip baptizing the Ethiopian eunuch. Legend has it that the apostle St Thomas – the doubting Thomas of John 20: 24–29 – had reached India and even that he had gone to China.

But the heartland of the faith was in the Roman Empire and along the border with Persia. It was here that the major developments took place. On the one hand, Christianity became more and more clothed in Greek philosophical language and imagery. On the other hand, there arose a mystery tradition – gnosticism – which veered away from this. The role of the gnostics in Christianity is a topic which engenders great debate and disagreement. As far as orthodoxy was, and is, concerned, they betrayed the truth of Christianity. Yet, while gnosticism certainly lost the battle to become the dominant form of Christianity, gnostic elements constantly reappear throughout history, and thus we need to look closely at what gnosticism was and why the official church rejected it.

THE GNOSTICS

The word 'gnostic' comes from the Greek *gnosis*, meaning knowledge. The central teaching of gnosticism was that the Bible, and Jesus himself, could be understood at two different levels. There was the simple, obvious one, and there was the secret one, open only to those who were initiated into the true meaning and mysteries of Christ and of the Bible. Gnostics point to Jesus having taught that there were different levels of meaning within his own parables. In Matthew 13: 10–17, Jesus explicitly says that some may know the mysteries of heaven and others not. The notion of a secret teaching or deeper meaning to the parables is thus verifiable within the gospels, yet the Church rejected this. Why?

The answer is that much of what the gnostics taught took certain key elements of the Christian story and gave them a radically different context. Whether in doing so, they were nearer to the truth of what Jesus meant, or whether they perverted the gospel, is what the debate was, and to some extent still is, all about.

Gnosticism taught that God was knowable through knowledge, the secret knowledge imparted by Jesus. It also taught that the material world was evil and a trap for the human soul. Indeed, not only was the world evil, but the human body was little more than a prison for the spark of the divine which was trapped within it. Having condemned the physical world as inherently evil, the gnostics developed a theology which explained the origin of the material world and its relationship to God. They claimed that the physical world had been created by a demiurge (a word taken from Platonic thought and meaning that which created the world). This demiurge had fallen from a state of true grace and existence within God and was thus in conflict with that which was truly spiritual. The world, the creation of this demiurge, was thus antagonistic to spiritual values. Because the demiurge seemed so powerful through its creation of the material world, people had mistakenly taken to worshipping the demiurge and calling it God, rather than worshipping and seeking to know the true God, who was beyond the material.

The idea for this demiurge came from the very real difficulties which early Christians had (and which many Christians have today) with the rather violent God of the Old Testament. Many found it difficult to reconcile the abstract Platonic notion of the divine – as expressed in part in the opening of St John's Gospel – with the God of the Israelites who smote the other nations, brought plagues to Egypt and misery on those who opposed him. The gnostic resolution was to say that the God encountered in the Old Testament was only this demiurge – which therefore could not be expected to be spiritual. The God revealed by Jesus, the gnostics claimed, was not the demiurge, but the true God, who was unconnected with the creation of the physical world. The role of Jesus was to bring knowledge – gnosis – of the true God and to cut a way through the false teachings of the demiurge and the Old Testament. However, only a few could ever free themselves sufficiently from the thrall of the material world to understand the secret knowledge brought by Jesus.

The gnostic denial of the value of the material world and their creation of the subsidiary god, the demiurge, places them outside orthodox theology. Yet for many years they were part of the various struggles and attempts to understand what Jesus Christ meant for the human race. They therefore had an impact on Christianity which was later to be picked up by Augustine. They taught Christianity to be suspicious of the material world, and in particular, of the physical body.

I am always amused when people in movements such as the environmental movement or human potential groups, romanticize the gnostics as if they were the true Christians who were suppressed by the orthodox. Given the teachings of the gnostics, which reject the material world and see it as inferior, even as evil, it is likely that the seeds of an anti-environmental, anti-sexual, anti-physical thread within Christianity owe as much to the gnostics as to any other 'heretical' group, if not more.

Variations of the gnostic tradition have reappeared throughout Christian history, partly because of the 'problem' of the Old Testament vision of God, and partly because of a tendency within Christianity to separate the physical from the spiritual. The Albigensians and Cathars of the eleventh to thirteenth centuries were, in part at least, manifestations of this gnostic view, considering as they did that the spirit world was created by one Principle (or Power), which was Good, and the material world was created by another Principle, which was Bad.

THE RISE OF EARLY MONASTICISM

Towards the end of the third century, Christianity, despite, or perhaps because of, many persecutions, had spread throughout society in the Roman Empire. Christianity was becoming the norm, especially in highly cosmopolitan and urbanized areas such as Alexandria. It was from such a setting that the first monastic tradition arose. In a deliberate rejection of the urbane and increasingly wealthy churches of Alexandria, people went out into the Egyptian desert to escape their corrupting influences and to commune with God in a more direct and intimate way. The greatest of these early monks was St Anthony, who moved further and further into the desert and established the harsh and demanding regime of fasting and prayer which was to be the hallmark of the hermit monks of the desert.

At times, the early monastic tradition seems to hover on the brink of a kind of gnosticism. The strong denial of the body and of the worth of all physical and bodily things, was often the flip side of the coin from the monks' desire to know God and to free the spirit from the tyranny of the body. However, most monks, kept within the confines of orthodox Christianity and brought to it a spirit of self-denial and intense prayer, which while it played down the importance of the physical, did not ultimately see it as an expression of an evil force or demiurge. There were communities of early Christians who did decide that the material world was evil and thus created by a force other than God, but they were expelled from the Church.

At times, the wandering monks caused great concern, for many of them were under no particular discipline. The right to be an independent monk has never ceased in the Eastern Churches, but as the third century moved into the momentous fourth century, St Pachomius established ordered communities of monks and nuns in the deserts of Egypt and drew up a rule by which they should live. From these beginnings come all the forms of monasticism within the Church, East or West. But also from them came a sense that the ascetic, celibate life was, when all was said and done, a more worthy and holy life than that of the married person living in the world. This strand has been a source of great inspiration to the Church, but it has also tended to make Christians view the body and the legitimate pleasures of the world as somewhat suspect.

THE CONVERSION OF THE STATE

The fourth to sixth centuries saw Christianity move from being one faith amongst others in the Roman world to being the official religion of the Empire and especially of its new form, Byzantium. It was also the period during which much of what we think of as classical Christianity was given its basic shape.

The period opens with Armenia becoming the first Christian state. It is an important reminder that Rome was not the first state to become officially Christian, and also that while its advances and successes within the Empire were very significant, Christianity had spread well beyond its borders. There were thriving churches in the Persian Empire, Arabia and India. Ireland was just beginning its own extraordinary Christian story (see Chapter 3) and as far east as Afghanistan, bishops were operating. Nor were all these churches under one authority. Increasingly the churches of the East had developed their own liturgies and canon of sacred texts. So Christianity was far from being just a Roman phenomenon. Indeed, until the conversion of Constantine, it was primarily a non-Roman religion, and its strongholds within the Empire were in the East – Egypt, Syria and the border lands of Persia.

In 312, the co-ruler of the Roman Empire, Constantine, marched on Rome against his co-ruler Maxentius. North of Rome, the armies clashed. As Constantine advanced with his army, he saw written in the sky, above a cross, the words *in hoc signo vinces* – 'By this sign, conquer.' Constantine defeated his opponent and the way thus lay open to Rome and to his taking total control of the Empire. Constantine believed that Christ had given him this victory and he immediately gave Christianity favoured status within the Empire, though he did not establish it as the official faith.

Under Constantine, the theory of Church and State as one was first articulated. Constantine saw himself as uniting both temporary and eternal power – the secular and the religious. To show that a new era had arrived, he established his capital at what was then known as Byzantium, renamed Constantinople in his honour. Here, away from the ancient temples and gods of Rome, a new city arose, founded upon Christianity. At its centre lay the palace and the cathedral. Here, the emperor, acting as ruler-priest, could call councils of the Church to decide religious and theological issues which were then enforced as state policy by state force or persuasion.

This state take-over or absorption of the Church is seen by many as the point at which true Christianity lost its freedom and vitality. Yet others see this time as being the era when Christianity began seriously to fulfil its role in the world. Certainly, Christianity in the Roman world was never quite the same after Constantine had tied the well being of the Empire to the vestments of the Church.

It was not until 380 that Theodosius actually declared Christianity to be the faith of the Empire. By that time, the faith had taken over all aspects of official life, despite a last ditch stand by the older Roman faith under Julian the Apostate. The fortunes of the Empire and of Christianity were seen to be intimately interwoven. This led to the persecution of Christians in neighbouring countries and empires, as they were suspected of being agents of the Roman Empire. But it also led heretical groups who were in dispute with the orthodox churches to seek the protection of these other countries and empires. This was a pattern which was to create great turmoil.

ST AUGUSTINE

A figure now appears on the scene whose theology and own life experiences had as dramatic an effect on the future direction of much of Roman Christianity as Constantine's conversion. His name was Augustine, and he was born in 354 in Thagaste, in modern-day Algeria and died in 430 as bishop of the north

African city of Hippo. It was from his writings that Roman Catholic theology took its main shape, a shape which also profoundly influenced the Protestant response. It is, however, important to stress here that Augustine had very little impact on the Eastern churches and none at all on those churches outside the Empire. The significance of this fact will be brought home when we look at different churches in Chapters 3 and 4.

Augustine's family encapsulated the pluralism of his times. His father was a pagan and his mother a Christian. He was brought up in a semi-Christian home but does not seem to have had much interest in Christianity. His days as a student and as a teacher were marked by a deeply loving relationship with a woman with whom he enjoyed a sort of family life, and by whom he had a son, Adeodatus. During this time, Augustine was greatly attracted by the teachings of Manichaeism. For ten years, from 373 to 383, he attended the meetings and discussions of this group. In 383 he went to Rome and there came under the influence of powerful Christian teachers, especially when he moved to Milan and met the bishop, St Ambrose.

His decision to seek baptism in 387 required him to forswear his mistress of some fifteen years, the mother of his son. This he very reluctantly did and was baptized on Easter Eve 387. He was ordained in 391, and spent the next four years as a monk. In 395 he was chosen, indeed almost forced, to become Bishop of Hippo, where he remained until his death in 430.

These are the bare bones of the life of Augustine. The particular way he chose to flesh them out was to stamp an indelible mark on Western Christianity.

His teachings were forged by a fascinating combination of controversy at a public level — much of his writing was in reaction to 'heretical' views — and the use of intensely personal experiences, especially in his famous *Confessions*. What has been an issue of continuing discussion in theological and historical circles has been the question of how orthodox he was. This may seem to be rather an odd question to ask about one of the great fathers of the Church. But is there a case for saying that Augustine distorted the teachings of the Church? Were Christian attitudes and beliefs different before and after Augustine in a way which makes a shift in thinking? Was Augustine actually unorthodox but so powerful in his teachings that what he taught became orthodoxy?

I would claim that they were. Augustine never really shook off the ideas he picked up from the Manichaeans. It is therefore important to look briefly at these.

MANICHAEISM

The founder of Manichaeism was Mani. He lived in Persia in the mid-third century and taught a faith which combined elements drawn from Christianity, Zoroastrianism, Buddhism, Hinduism and a range of other beliefs. The core of his teaching was a reworking of the Zoroastrian dualism. He taught that the whole of creation was caught up in a vast cosmic battle between the forces of good and evil, light and dark. In language often similar to that of the gnostics, he taught that the soul was a spark of the good, of the light, which had been trapped by the evil forces of darkness and imprisoned in the body. The whole point of religion, argued Mani, was to help free the trapped particles of light and thus reunite them with the Ultimate Good. This, claimed Mani, was what the great teachers − Zoroaster, the prophets, Jesus, the Buddha and others − had all come to teach.

The practice of Manichaeism reflected this suspicion of the body and the physical world. Extreme asceticism and chastity were its hallmarks, along with different grades or levels of knowledge. Augustine himself never moved much beyond the lowest levels, but he was attracted by this faith, as were many others both in the Roman Empire and beyond. For a while it looked as if Manichaeism might be a genuine rival to Christianity, but it soon declined.

Augustine never seems to have fully shaken off this dualistic attitude, nor his sense that the physical world was bad. It is true that when writing against the Manichaeans in later life, he stoutly defended the innate goodness of all creation and thus the goodness of God who had created all life. Yet, if he could, at least in theory, be positive about the rest of creation, he never saw humanity as particularly good. The asceticism and fear of sex which was a mark of Manichaeism seem to have passed on into his Christianity, but in a mixed and emotive way. Augustine had enjoyed the good life – things of life – his mistress or common-law wife, good food, and the like. When he had to turn away from his mistress on becoming a Christian, he seems to have tried very hard to reject the pleasures of the body and of the world. But he was constantly attracted 'Give me chastity and continence, but not yet' (Confessions VIII. 7) was one of his *cris de cœur*. In the *Confessions* he grappled with this in a way which is as moving today as it was in the fifth century. But in the end, Augustine bequeathed to the Church in the West a guilt complex about sexuality and pleasure which has served it ill. This, combined with certain aspects of the gnostic rejection of the body and the asceticism and anti-pleasure principles of the monks, gave Western Christianity a very strong anti-world, anti-body, anti-sexuality and anti-women bias. It is one which many in the churches today are struggling to reinterpret. It is a major source of critical comments about Christianity, and I would claim that much of what Augustine taught has led influential sections of the Western Church down paths which it did not need to explore and has diverted us away from more legitimate concerns.

Pelagius and the Issue of Human Nature

One of the great debates that Augustine engaged in was on the nature of humanity: on what kind of being we are in our essence. One approach to this fundamental question arises from the teachings of the fourth–fifth-century British monk, Pelagius. In a series of books and public debates he argued that human nature is basically good. He believed that human beings are capable of good deeds and actions that in themselves help in the process of full salvation. But he also recognized that humanity can be misled and that evil actions thus arise.

However, he strongly attacked anything that removed from us responsibility for our own actions, either good or bad. In line with Jewish thought, he did not believe that humanity had been eternally blighted by Adam's sin, but rather that all people are born free of sin and it is thus our duty to take responsibility for our own actions. Essentially, Pelagius' model is an optimistic one with regard to human nature and its potential. It is a view which has actually been held in many of its aspects by many Christians down the ages and by certain branches of the Church, such as much of the Church of the Eastern Roman world and beyond that into the churches of Persia and the lands beyond. But in the Western Church, Pelagius lost the argument to Augustine.

Augustine's approach was very different, and he was Pelagius' most vehement opponent and he preached and wrote against him. Augustine took a much more pessimistic view of humanity. He felt that the fall of Adam had not just robbed humanity of its virtues and power for good, but that through original sin, all human beings were born tainted. This sin manifested itself in a basic disposition to rebel against God's will. Augustine referred to humanity as 'one mass of sin', and he saw God's grace as being the only way we can be lifted above the inherent wickedness and rebelliouness of our nature. A result of Augustine's view was that he held that people would never behave well from their own volition. Therefore he sanctioned the role of civic authorities in keeping control and in making people behave in at least a moderately civilized way. Deviation from this standard could thus be punished by the State, as he believed the State to be divinely appointed by God to instil a sense of right and wrong into sinful humanity. This did not mean that the State could play any religious role, merely that it could control the excesses of human behaviour.

Augustine lived at a time of immense social unrest – in fact, a time not unlike our own when old established power blocks, empires and alliances were crumbling. In 410, Rome was sacked by the Visigoths and the Roman world seemed to be staggering to its last days in the West. It looked as if the partnership of Church and State was doomed. No sooner had the Empire gone Christian, argued contemporaries and opponents of Augustine, than the Empire fell.

Augustine's response to this was his magnificent work, *The City of God*. Here he presented a picture of the city which is of God, an everlasting city in contrast to the fallen and defeated city of humanity, especially of Rome. In doing so, he played, albeit in a novel way, on the theme of the good spiritual world pitted against flawed if not actually bad physical world. His Manichaean background played a strong subcurrent role in shaping his views, although he of course denied this.

It is this semi-Manichaean disgust with the physical world which led him to postulate the City of God as the model. The City of God is a new community, not affected or influenced by the reality of cities here on earth. Augustine, heir to a triumphant Christianity which had seized the social and political high ground, had had to face the collapse of many sections of the social and political world which the faith now controlled. He had had to withstand the jeers of those who said that it was Christianity which had brought about the disasters which now beset the Empire. His response, in line with the Manichaean teachings he studied for so long, led him to spiritualize the notion ot the true city or domain of the Christian.

Augustine also strengthened another emerging trend within the Church. Society had not been redeemed by the success of Christianity. What did this mean in terms of the roles of the Church and society? It was Augustine who first clearly articulated the idea that outside the Church there was no salvation. In other words, the Church itself was the only society and community which could offer any salvation. Anything which was not the Church was beyond the pale, even if it was in a society largely controlled by the Church. Augustine's theology gave the Church itself a power and authority, an absolutism, which had never been articulated quite so powerfully before.

THE FAITH SPREADS

While Augustine and Pelagius were arguing about human nature, the churches outside the Roman world were expanding rapidly. In Ethiopia, the first fully recorded growth of Christianity came in the fourth century under Saints Frumentius and Edesius of Tyre, later followed by the Nine Roman (meaning Byzantine) Saints sent from the Syrian Church. By the fifth century, the first great cathedral had been built in the capital city, Axum, and Ethiopia was lending spiritual and military assistance to other churches and fledgling Christian states such as that which was flourishing in what is now the Yemen.

In 525, the Ethiopians invaded the Yemen in order to crush a pro-Persian Jewish ruler who was reportedly oppressing native Christians. By the mid-sixth century, the vast cathedral in the city of Sana'a was a centre of popular pilgrimage second only to the Kaaba in Mecca – then still a pagan shrine. From Sana'a, Christianity spread up into the Arabian peninsular and by the end of the sixth century a number of highly powerful and influential Arab tribes, such as the Ghassan, had converted.

Meanwhile, in Persia and beyond, a variety of Christianity had taken hold which was opposed to the formal faith of the Roman Empire. Nestorianism was by the end of the sixth century, on its way to being as big numerically and certainly as widespread geographically as Roman or Byzantine Christianity. Its influence stretched from India to the borders of China, from the Russian steppes to the banks of the Euphrates.

I look in detail at the Nestorian Church in Chapter 4, so I shall only say a little here. The ancient orthodox Church of mainstream Christianity had to face two very different kinds of stresses in its journey from the disciples gathered together at Pentecost to the end of the sixth century. First, what was deemed to be 'orthodox' emerged from a vast array of conflicting schools and teachings in which some, like the Jewish Church were easily sidelined, while others, like the gnostics and Manichaeans formed para-Churches of their own. On the whole, orthodox Christianity found these alternative churches relatively easy either to marginalize or to cast out of the main body of Christianity, so fundamentally different and at variance were their teachings. Perhaps an example would be the relationship between the present-day Protestant churches and the Church of Unification, the sect of the Rev. Moon, known as the Moonies. Whilst sharing certain terms, figures and even scriptures, the interpretation placed upon these same areas and the status given to Rev. Moon places the Church of Unification firmly outside standard Christianity.

Of greater difficulty were those differences which reflected relatively minor theological shifts or stances, but which were linked to socio-political forces at work within the vast geographical and racial spread of the faith. Of these, the Arian, Monophysite and Nestorian controversies were the most significant in both aiding and hindering the spread of the faith.

OF HERESIES, ARIANS, NESTORIANS AND MONOPHYSITES

Arius lived from about 250 to 335 and came from Alexandria. He taught that Christ was not an eternal part of the godhead, but had been brought into being by the Father in order both to create and to redeem the world. As such, Christ became an instrument of God in Arius's thinking, rather than an equal part of the divine. Arianism, as his beliefs came to be known, split the Roman/Byzantine Empire, and for nearly seventy years, from the early to the late fourth century dominated church debates and greatly influenced Church/State relations. Several emperors of the East favoured Arianism and persecuted the more orthodox believers. This began to lay the seeds for dissent amongst those on the edge of the Byzantine world whose faith now seemed to be dictated more by rulers than by priests. This disaffection was to provide fertile ground for later developments and splits. In particular, the wavering of the Eastern emperors, based at Constantinople, had led the Roman-centred churches to look askance at Constantinople and the Byzantine rulers. This alienation from Constantinople was further increased by the invasions of Italy in the early fifth century and onwards, when Constantinople proved incapable of defending Rome.

The Church survived the Arian controversy and the teaching that God and Christ are of the same divinity came to be orthodox teaching: 'very God of very God' as the Nicene creed, drawn up in 525 to refute Arianism, states. While certain Germanic tribes were to remain Arian in their beliefs for more than two hundred years (until the late fifth and early sixth centuries), orthodoxy re-established itself, but it had been badly shaken and cracks had appeared which had as much to do with a local desire for autonomy and resentment of imperial control as with theology.

The next two disagreements caused splits in mainstream Christianity, some of which have not to this day been healed.

Nestorius was Bishop of Constantinople from 428 to 431. In 431 he was deposed at the instigation of the Patriarch of Alexandria, Cyril. The reasons for Nestorius' deposition was that he objected to the use of the term 'Mother of God' for the Virgin Mary. For Nestorius, this detracted from the real humanity of Jesus Christ and placed too much emphasis on his divinity. The Council of Ephesus in 431 condemned Nestorius' views as heretical and expelled him. But this did not end the affair. Far from it. As we shall see in the chapter on the Nestorians, the Eastern church, the church outside the confines of the Byzantine Empire, took Nestorian ideas to its heart and became no longer in communion with the Western or Byzantine church.

This was a very useful move, for it meant that the non-Byzantine church was no longer seen as a fifth column by the great rival of Byzantium, the Persian Empire. Once the Persian and parts of the Syrian churches had become Nestorian and were thus no longer linked to Constantinople, the Persians could view them with indifference or as allies against the force and power of the orthodox Christian empire of Byzantium. The freedom from suspicion and the access to distant parts along the Persian trade routes which thus opened up, led to the Nestorian church's growth to become second only to the Byzantine Church in size and power; it was also the most widely spread church in the ancient world.

Ironically, it was because of over-reaction in Alexandria to the humanizing ideas of Christ put forward by Nestorius that the next major split occurred. In seeking to emphasize the divinity of Christ in order to 'correct' the Nestorian imbalance, the Patriarch of Alexandria, Dioskorus (444–454) stressed the divinity of Christ almost to the point of denying his humanity. He taught that there was just one nature present in Christ, the divine; humanity and divinity were not combined in him, as orthodoxy taught. Because his followers taught just one nature, they became known as the Monophysites – one-nature believers. After various sordid intrigues and wrangles, the emperor and the Patriarch of Constantinople called a council at Chalcedon, on the Asian coast opposite Constantinople in 451. This council denounced Monophysite beliefs as heretical.

But this did not have the expected result. Whereas Nestorianism had gone off into the non-Byzantine areas, the Monophysites took over great sections of the Byzantine world. The vast majority of the Egyptian church became Monophysite and formed what is now known as the Coptic church. Likewise, the Ethiopian church went Monophysite. As these two churches soon passed (in the mid-seventh century) under Arab Muslim rule, they were protected from the wrath of the emperors. The next church to become Monophysite was the Syrian, already feeling estranged and vunerable because of its perilous position on the borders between Byzantium and Persia. Finally the Armenians became Monophysite, again to some degree seeking to hold a balance between their masters in Constantinople and the Persian and later Muslim forces on their other flank.

These churches not only left orthodoxy, as defined by Constantinople and Rome, when they went Monophysite. With the exception of Armenia they also left the protection and authority of a Christian state. In doing so, they were in a good position to weather the storm of the invasion of Islam in the mid-seventh century. They also had to develop an indigenous faith which reflected the cultural setting in which they found themselves. Only now are we beginning to discover the riches and insights which the Coptic, Syrian and Ethiopian churches have developed, cut off from Western Christianity for so many centuries. Many of the developments in theology which have deeply scarred or enabled the Western church had no influence whatsoever over these Monophysite or Nestorian churches. This is important to recall, for many of the strands which

which have made people today most wary of Christianity are virtually unknown in these great ancient churches.

THE CHURCHES AT THE END OF THE SIXTH CENTURY

Let us take stock at this point. Christianity, by the end of the sixth century had become the formal faith of the Roman Empire. That Empire had effectively fragmented into two main sections, the West, now overrun by barbarian tribes, many of whom were converting to Christianity, and the East where a Christian empire had clearly taken shape. Theologically, the Western church had developed out of the chaos a systematic way of understanding its position *vis-à-vis* the State which elevated the spiritual world above the social, material one. In the East, monasticism had performed a similar task, not in a systematic way, as in the West, but by example. However, the Byzantine state saw itself and the Church as partners in Christendom. In the West, the Church saw itself as supreme, and as time went on, it helped create or sanctify, new kingdoms and groupings.

Theologically, the Church had shed many different forms of Christianity. Some had taken themselves off, as Jewish Christianity and to a certain degree, the gnostics did. Others had been forced out, like the Pelagians, Monophysites and the Nestorians. Yet others had established a precarious hold on the edges of mainstream Christianity – the Celtic church was just beginning, and monasticism was starting to assert its distinctive understanding of the Christian life. Major new churches had come into being well beyond the borders of the official Christian state of Rome. These churches were not linked to the State and were free to develop their teachings as a religious minority rather than as the spiritual wing of a secular power. However, the Roman/Byzantine church was beginning to understand itself, society and human nature in various ways, ways that were to end with schism at the end of the millennium.

What is important to remember is that throughout this period, ordinary Christians were finding a sense of belonging, of community and of communion with God which was shaping their lives. Furthermore, this period was a remarkable one for the power of Christian social teaching. The writings of the church fathers on economics still provide some of the most dramatic insights into the religious life and economics imaginable. St John Chrysostom (c. 347–407) is far from unusual:

> Tell me then, how did you come to be rich? Who gave you all this, and where did he get it from? From his father and grandfather – but can you show, going back through the generations, that such ownership was got by just means? It can never have been. The root and origin of it all must have been injustice. Why? Because God in the beginning did not make one person wealthy and another poor. Nor did he afterwards show one person great treasures of gold and, deny the other the right to know about such treasures. He left the earth free to all alike. Why, then, if it is common, have you so many acres of land, while your neighbour has none at all?
>
> (Homily 12 on I Timothy)

Likewise, much of the Church's teachings on the environment stressed the fact that God had created all to be equal and to share the riches of the creation in common.

Where orthodox Christianity was getting into hot water was on the issues of sexuality, women and the body. The strong anti-material dimension within Platonic thought and within heresies such as gnosticism and Manichaeism, led Christianity into treating the material world as at least suspect. The rise of the monastic tradition, while stressing the communal, anti-wealth teachings of the Church, also gave celibacy a status which it had not had before. The celibacy of priests is quite a late idea in the Roman Catholic church and has never applied to the Orthodox priests, unless they are monks. This notion of celibacy gave greater emphasis to the idea that sex was in some basic way wrong. This in turn led many church fathers to view woman as the temptress who lured man into sex and away from a pure life.

There was also the rise of guilt. Augustine took what is a perfectly natural part of Christianity – the idea that one should repent of one's sins and start again, and turned this into guilt.

His *Confessions* read today as if they were written by a modern Christian. This is largely because so many of us have been conditioned to think about ourselves and our guilt in ways set by Augustine. But the early Church was not a guilt-ridden Church. Far from it. The Church saw itself as proclaiming a message of freedom from guilt, a releasing of the individual to be part of the kingdom of God. On this score, study of early eucharistic liturgies is interesting. The word 'eucharist' means 'thanksgiving.' The whole emphasis of the early church through eucharist was to thank God for the world, for Jesus Christ, for freedom and for the coming of the community of the kingdom – the fellowship of Christians. While acknowledgement of failings was a part of the preparation, it was a corporate acknowledgement and was a very minor part of the service.

Look today at an Anglican or Roman Catholic service and confessions of sin, guilt and unworthiness are a significant part of the service. Read any biography of a lapsed Catholic and the thing they complain about most is the guilt complex that was instilled in them. The same is true of extreme Protestants. It is at Augustine's feet that we need to lay at least some of the blame for this, and especially the link between sex and guilt. As we shall see in chapters 6 and 7, this development did not take place in other churches, nor is it a feature of orthodoxy today; a sense of being unworthy, yes, but not this wallowing in sin and guilt.

The question of the nature of humanity was also being hammered out during these centuries. The debate between Augustine and Pelagius is but the most vivid illustration of this. What does it mean to be human? Does it mean we are wicked and need saving, or that we are children of God who need to be called back to the Father? Was it inevitable that fallen humanity should attack and kill love incarnate, Jesus Christ? Or was the passion of Christ a terrible reminder of how we should behave, without fear and suspicion but with love and compassion? The nature of the early Christian communities was such that outsiders said, 'See how these Christians love one another.' The communality of goods and life was also a mark of many sections of the Church – and was of course expressed most forcefully through the communal life of the monks and nuns. Yet within a few centuries, the Church in the Roman Empire was accruing to itself vast wealth and power.

On the issue of Jesus' question 'Who do people say that I am?' the Church was vacillating between stressing the divine and stressing the human – arriving via the Nicene creed with a formula which held both together, in paradox. Yet this same debate about the divine and the human in Christ continues to this day among people both within and outside the churches.

In terms of the relationships between Church and State within the Roman Empire and its fragments, two distinct models were emerging: one was of the Church and State operating as one for the common good; the other was of the Church alone ensuring the good and the State acting as an adjunct to this, but without being ultimately as important because it could not offer any hope. Salvation lay within the Church alone. Outside the Roman world, the Church faced a wide range of different situations from being in a majority but without state power to being a persecuted minority.

THE RISE OF ISLAM

In the seventh century, much of the Christian world was turned upside down by the rise of Islam and its invasions. The Middle East and North Africa, areas which had been almost totally Christian were within less than a hundred years, converting to Islam to the extent that Christianity either disappeared completely or found itself a minority religion in its own lands. The speed of the spread of Islam had many causes. The power of its teaching about one God was very attractive to a world grown weary of endless debates about the exact nature of the Trinity as between the Orthodox and the Monophysites or the Nestorians. The authority of Islam also appealed to those who resented the authority of Constantinople, and to a much lesser extent, Rome. The violence of Islam also persuaded many that acceptance was preferable to death. However, the outcome was roughly the same. For very understandable reasons, Islam came

to represent everthing which was against Christianity, theologically, socially and politically. Islam took up its role as enemy
number one of the Church and the West, a role which it has
maintained almost without break, except during the Reformation when Catholics had the Protestants to despise and vice
versa, and the period during the twentieth century when Communism took over as the bogey man.

With the coming of Islam, Christianity began to develop
again the apocalyptic notions which had so inspired its early
writers at the time when the Roman state was the enemy.
Struggling against the foe now became a Christian duty.

It is easy to shake one's head in disbelief, living this far from
the events. Yet that would be unfair. The onslaught of the first
rush of Islam was terrible. The ravages on the coastlines of
Greece, Turkey and Italy in the seventh and eighth centuries left
areas so depopulated and destroyed that many cities, let alone
towns and villages, never rose again. On the island of Crete,
only one church survives from the time before the first rise of
Islam – a small church hidden away in the hills. Every other
building was levelled to the ground. Christianity was literally
fighting for its life and in particular the Byzantine empire,
combining Church and State as one, saw the attacks on its
territory as equally an attack on the faith. The fact that the
Christian communities, were often well treated after the
invasions, does not remove the initial terror of the slaughter and
violence.

From now on, Christianity in the old Roman and new Byzantium empires had to take account of the challenge, theological
as well as military, of Islam. In the East, beyond the confines of
the Byzantine Empire, Christians had to learn to live as minorities within cultures which they had once ruled (Egypt and
North Africa), or as communities which had never had power
but were now under the aegis of a faith-based state, not unlike
the faith state of Byzantium (Persia, Arabia and much of the
Middle East). Thus, one strand of the Church had to develop a
military response, while another could not. The impact of this
on the mindset of the different worlds is profound and is still to
be seen to this day.

THE ELEVENTH CENTURY AND ITS THEOLOGY

We take a leap in time now to the eleventh century. During this century the schism between the Byzantine and the Roman churches was formally recognized in the so-called Great Schism of 1054. This marks the date when emissaries of the Pope placed an order (bull) of excommunication on the Patriarch of Constantinople. From then on the two major halves of Christendom were barely on speaking terms. Their development continued in the very different ways which have been outlined above.

This century also saw a shift in Christian understanding of the meaning of Christ's life in the Western/Roman church, which was to distance the two churches further. The church fathers had debated the meaning of Christ's life, death and resurrection along two main lines. The first, which was ultimately discredited within the Orthodox churches, was that Christ had died as a ransom to the devil by which he bought all the souls whom the devil had captured, or might capture. It was this view which was largely adopted in the West and which functioned as a basic model for many Roman Catholic missions reaching out into pagan areas. They found the idea of a struggle against the forces of darkness very appealing, as indeed did many of their converts. Meanwhile, in the East, this idea was put aside in favour of the view of Christ as our representative. He exemplifies what we are all capable of, if we dwell in God. Indeed, St Anthenasius (c. 296–373) went so far as to state that God became man so that man might become God. This statement, devoid of any dualism or sense of the devil being in control, expresses the idea of Christ as a model for life rather than an offering.

In the West, the semi-dualism of the devil as hostage-taker was gradually played down. Instead, God was recentred as the only cosmic and eternal force with which humanity had to deal. The belief arose that the sins of humanity were eternal ones – deriving from Adam and being marked upon all human beings. As such, there is nothing that any individual can do to cleanse themselves from this original sin. A sin – the sin of Adam which to this day Jews find one of the most incomprehensible of Christian teachings – had marred all humanity for ever. Humanity was seen to be polluted beyond redemption by it.

St Anselm, Archbishop of Canterbury at the end of the eleventh century, put forward a new understanding of the role of Christ in the light of these ideas. He taught that sin is an eternal consequence of being human and as such cannot be eradicated by human action. Therefore only the eternal could take upon itself the oppression of sin and its consequences and overcome it. Anselm taught that God could not absolve the terrible consequences of human sin. Instead, Anselm saw Jesus Christ coming and taking upon himself sin, past, present and future, and overcoming it by paying the ultimate price – death. In this model, Anselm sets God up as an immovable judge of justice. Having set the conditions, God finds himself unable to forgive humanity, for to do so would be to lessen his justice. Thus, Jesus Christ came to take our sins upon himself, and thus to be killed – in a sense by God, or at least for God – in order that the eternal nature of sin might be broken. Jesus took upon himself the death which was God's punishment for sin.

This, to my mind horrific, theology is called substitutionary atonement. In it Jesus, far from ransoming souls from the devil, rescues them from the Father. The model of the angry, unforgiving God who demands blood and a life, even if it is his own son's, has deeply damaged Christianity in my opinion and runs contrary both to what the other major churches teach and to what the gospels themselves present as the meaning and purpose of Jesus Christ.

Fortunately, much of Western Christianity has always found this view to be abhorrent, yet it built upon the Augustinian legacy of guilt to produce an understanding of Christianity which dwelt upon fear and worthlessness, and which was to arise in yet more complex forms in the Reformation. In contrast, Abelard (1079–1142) taught that the basis of the incarnation, life, death and resurrection of Christ was love. By seeing what humanity did to love when Christ was nailed to the cross, Christ evokes within the Christian a similar love, which is then the redeeming power which removes sin from us and gives us a model to follow. Abelard saw sin as being simply but dramatically the failure to follow the wishes of God. Hence he did not believe in a blood atonement nor in a dualistic struggle between good and evil. Rather he saw Christ as the supreme example of humanity obeying the will of God – regardless of the cost.

THE CRUSADES

Meanwhile, elsewhere, Christianity was spreading further north. Russia became a Christian nation in 988 and missions pushed into Scandinavia. Islam had been checked by the Byzantines and the Spanish, but then came the notion of the crusades. The First Crusade was launched in 1095 and for 300 years it shaped not just the lives of the Western Catholic Christians who went to fight and to gain kingdoms, but also the lives of the Orthodox Christians and others of the East who got in the way! Many Orthodox and Eastern Christians had grown used to living under the rule of Islam. Famous theologians of the Orthodox church such as John of Damascus were actually officials in the court of the Muslim rulers. Occasionally, violence or oppression would erupt against the Christians, but on the whole, life was liveable.

The crusades helped Western Europe deal with overpopulation and the energies of the young men who sought to create new kingdoms and fiefdoms for themselves. It was also a genuinely sincere attempt to win back the sacred places of Christianity – at least at first. It was also the first sign of an arrogant and intolerant strand within Western Christianity, which was to be one of the foundations upon which colonialism and racism were built. The West began by treating the Eastern churches as equals in the venture. However, it soon became clear that it had little interest in helping them recover their lost provinces. Indeed, no sooner did the crusaders take cities such as Antioch and Jerusalem than they appointed their own clergy and established the Roman Catholic church instead of the original Orthodox churches.

By the beginning of the thirteenth century the target had changed. The Fourth Crusade never even tried to get to the Holy Land. Instead, it turned aside and attacked Constantinople. The first fall of Constantinople in the 1204 was an orgy of destruction from which the city never recovered, even though the Byzantines recaptured it in 1268. The intolerance of the crusaders for a different form of Christianity was mirrored in their persecution of the Jewish communities within their own countries. The rise of violent anti-Semitism stems from the time of the crusades when the enemy without was also feared to be the enemy within. The notion that the world was in thrall to demonic forces, arising from certain interpretations of the scriptures, and the theory of atonement based upon Christ ransoming humanity from the devil, laid theological foundations which were built upon by the genuine fear of Islam. The fear of the Jews came from this same source. If the devil was an ever-present force, ready to strike when least expected, then surely the Jews were the agents of such a force? For, the theologians argued, they had not only killed Jesus and persecuted the early Christians, but they had also failed to recognize their wickedness, and thus they should be considered as a fifth column, a constant rebel group in the heart of Christendom. Furthermore, some preachers accused the Jews of Satanism and of taking the blood of Christian babies to make unleavened bread. Many of Europe's phobias and fears were projected onto the Jews.

It cannot be stressed too strongly that the roots of the racism and imperialism of Western Christianity only really date from the time of the crusades. Prior to that, the seeds had been sown, but it took the extraordinary circumstances of the crusades, the early stirrings of nation states bolstered by a national church identity and the pogroms against the Jews, such as the mass destructions of Jewish communities all down the Rhine during the First Crusade, to bring them to full growth.

Again, I would remind you that this was only one face of Christianity. The Eastern churches were living very different theologies. In the West, the eleventh century saw the beginnings of a vast revival and expansion of the monastic tradition. Here Christianity showed its face of love, for almost all monasteries had hospitals and leprosariums, and provided shelter and food for the homeless and itinerant. The monasteries also provided centres of education which sought to explore not just Christian theology but also the writings of the philosophers and others from antiquity. Nor were all Christians gung-ho crusaders. Many refused to take the cross and did not support such wars. But the 'might equals right' lobby was gaining ground and the next 300 years saw an extraordinary development with, on the one hand the violence of the crusades and the murderous assaults upon heretics such as the Albigensians, and on the other the appearance of figures like St Francis and St Thomas Aquinas.

THOMAS AQUINAS

The story of Thomas Aquinas is a fascinating one because it is the earliest recorded attempt at deprogramming! Aquinas came from a wealthy and highly influential Italian family. Born in 1225, his family wanted him to become a powerful abbot in the Benedictine order. Instead, in 1241 he decided to join the new, mendicant and decidedly poor order of the Dominicans. His family were appalled, so much so that, in a pattern now used by those trying to deprogramme members of 'cults', they kidnapped him. They kept him locked up on the family estate for fifteen months while they tried to break his resolve. This included sending attractive young ladies into his room for the night. But Thomas held true to his calling and eventually the family had to relent.

Aquinas' great work was the *Summa Theologica*, in which he interwove Christian theology with Aristotelian thought. The works of Aristotle on philosophy had only recently been rediscovered and thus there was much fascination with his ideas. In a nutshell, what Aquinas did was to draw upon Aristotelian thought to give a massive structure of systematic theology to Christian teachings in the West. It must be remembered that his writings had virtually no impact on the Eastern churches, who held that there was nothing new to say about Christian theology.

Aquinas postulated a clear divide, and indeed a hierarchy, between faith and reason. Following Aristotle, he agreed that many aspects of life were capable of reasoned exploration and understanding. Indeed, not to act reasonably was to deny a part of being human. But he saw reason as having limitations, and of being ultimately of secondary importance. For there are certain areas of truth which cannot be arrived at by reason, only by faith. On issues such as the existence of God or the understanding of the incarnation, Aquinas points out that reason cannot help and that for a knowledge of such truths, we have to rely instead on faith in the revelations of God made in the Bible and in Christ, and expounded by the church fathers.

In his own way, Aquinas was the final actor in the long process of making Greek thought and philosophy a suitable vehicle for Christian insights. As such, he marks the end of Western Christianity's attempts to handle the pluralism of the early Church, between the Hebraic and Greek worlds.

At almost the same time that Aquinas was completing one struggle with pluralism, St Francis was exploring other forms.

ST FRANCIS

In its missionary work, the Church, and especially the Western church, had seen pantheism — belief that there were deities present within the natural world, or that the natural world was divine in its own right — as one of its greatest foes. Opposition to the nature worship of the pagan tribes had moulded Christian thought over many centuries. It had given perhaps undue emphasis to the notion that creation was not, in and of itself, sacred. Instead, Christianity had stressed the ordinariness of the rest of creation. If you sought God in nature, nature would not tell you much. Instead you should seek him in Christ and in the Church.

St Francis emerged at a time when the threat of the pagan, pantheistic world had receded. He sought therefore to resacralize all of creation by incorporating it within the family of God

– sacredness by association, if you like. Francis spoke of all elements of creation, from the sun and the moon to the birds, as being his brothers and sisters. In doing so, he was rejecting the anti-material aspects of certain forms of the Christian invective against pantheism. In modern parlance, he was expressing a much more holistic vision of both God and the meaning and purpose of creation. But he was in one sense a voice crying in the wilderness.

Ironically, his vision of all creation as part of God, yet with God greater than all creation, was one of the fundamental triggers of scientific research. With Aquinas stressing the use of reason in many areas, but especially in the natural sciences, and with Francis stressing that all life was of God, scientific exploration began. For, if God is in all creation and one loves God, then what better way of knowing more about God than knowing more about creation? Added to this is the fact that the Dominicans and Franciscans took the monk out of the cloister and on to the paths and roads of Europe. Travelling across widely diverse landscapes, they observed nature, in many different forms, at first hand rather than reading about it. From this intertwining of Aristotelian ideas of knowledge and the mendicant, wandering life of these monks, came the search after knowledge and truth expressed by the early scientists. Roger Bacon and William Ockham, living in the thirteenth century, were both early scientists and Franciscans. The impact of the rise of science on the West was of course to be enormous. It is the particular fate of Western Christianity that it alone of all the churches should have produced this fulcrum from which the scientific enterprise arose.

THE CHURCHES OF THE EAST

In the East, the period up to the end of the fourteenth century was marked by the continuing decline of the Byzantine Empire and the comings and goings of the crusades and the various Muslim groupings. The Nestorian church reached its peak in the middle of the fourteenth century. At that time it had twenty-five archbishops (called metropolitans), with some 250 dioceses spread from Peking to Persia and from Outer Mongolia to India, with roughly fifteen million believers. In churches such as the Nestorians and the Monophysite/Syrians, churches which in most cases were without state support, little had changed for centuries. The same was also true for many of the officially Orthodox churches (for the Nestorians and Monophysites also see themselves as Orthodox). Orthodoxy holds that the core teachings of the faith have been given in the Bible and the great church fathers. Basically, after the ninth century, anything new was simply a gloss on older teachings. The idea of a Thomas Aquinas was inconceivable. What was common throughout the Eastern churches was the role of the saint or holy person whose life was a shining example of what being a Christian meant.

In 1380, the Mongolian hordes of Tamerlane (Timur the Lame) burst out of Mongolia. Within twenty years they had destroyed all the great cities and ancient civilizations in a vast swathe from northern China, through northern India and Persia to the edge of Palestine itself. Millions upon millions of people were slaughtered or died as a result of the total breakdown of society. In this inferno of destruction, many of the ancient Eastern churches were snuffed out, completing what the coming of Islam had begun in certain areas.

From the beginning of the fifteenth century, Christianity was largely a European and Russian phenomenon, with remnant communities in Egypt, throughout the Middle East and further afield in India and some parts of what is today Iraq. In 1453, the great Christian city of Constantinople fell to the Turks. With the death of the last emperor, dying in defence of his city, the Byzantine Empire ended and most of the Greek Orthodox world passed into the hands of the Muslims. Limited to keeping alive their tradition within a hostile environment, the Eastern churches did not play a major role in world Christianity for many centuries to come.

Russia, however, was still free, and was to have an impact. Seeing itself as the third Rome (following Constantinople's claim to be the second Rome), it sought to protect and also dominate the Orthodox world, from the sheltered world of Mt

Athos to the wastes of Siberia. Starting in the sixteenth century, the Russian Orthodox church expanded rapidly across the vast tracts of Siberia. In this conquest/conversion, second only to the Roman Catholic expansion in Latin America, Orthodoxy established a folk faith of immense power and popularity. Absorbing shamanistic tribes, Orthodoxy in Russia became yet more mystical and produced some of the most remarkable iconography and spiritual writings of the period. Eventually the momentum of the missionary movement of Russian Orthodoxy washed up on the shores of Alaska and California in the late eighteenth and early nineteenth centuries.

THE PRELUDE TO THE REFORMATION

But it was Western Christianity which from the fifteenth century onwards was to be the focal point of Christianity and, as we have seen, it had been developing some very distinctive teachings, even if for the vast majority of the faithful, loving adherence to the faith of Christ was what kept them going. Indeed, it is interesting to note that it was to Christianity, or forms of Christianity, that people turned for justification when armed rebellions sprang up amongst the peasants and workers of Europe. A classic case is the Peasants' Revolution of 1382 in England. This rebellion saw the killing of an archbishop and chief justice and was only controlled by tricking the peasants into believing that their grievances concerning lack of land and basic rights of assembly and work would be dealt with. Its basic premise, that God had created all equal, was captured in a popular jingle of the time: 'When Adam delved and Eve span, who was then the gentleman?'

As we come to the fifteenth century, so we come to a period of unparalleled developments in Europe and within Western Christianity. The two engines of these developments were the intellectual and artistic advances of the Renaissance and the theological and religious developments of the Reformation.

The Renaissance, with its rediscovery of Greek and Latin ideas, plus the rise of the new humanist understanding of humanity – man is the measure of all things – was fuelled in part by the collapse of the Greek empire of Byzantium and eventually by the fall of Constantinople in 1453. Scholars fled West carrying precious volumes, and began to teach Western scholars Greek. The rediscovery of so much ancient knowledge and the reappraisal of classical civilization in general led many within the artistic and intellectual circles of Europe to question many of the claims of Christianity and to elevate humanity to a new position, a new mastery over life.

The Renaissance, whilst deeply rooted in Western Christianity, was also a reaction to the negative, pessimistic view of humanity which Western Christianity had often presented. It is not without significance that Thomas More, chancellor under Henry VIII and martyr for Catholicism, was also a leading humanist and wrote *Utopia*. The vision of society in this work assumed a human society capable of sensible self-regulation and of a degree of perfectibility of lifestyle. It was in stark contrast to, say, Augustine's *City of God*. More's vision assumes a humanity capable of greater learning, organization and compassion. His optimism for the human race stands in contrast to Augustine's faith only in God as being able to redeem or reform human society.

Meanwhile the Roman Catholic church at the end of the fifteenth century was in a terrible mess. Corruption, vice and decay were the hallmarks of large swathes of the church. The farce of the rival popes – one in Avignon supported by the French, with another in Rome whose supporters included the Holy Roman Empire, England and Spain – which had gone on from 1378 to 1417 had greatly weakened the papacy and in particular had made each of the rival claimants dependent upon kings and states. This had turned on its head the model of Church and State which the Western church had so assiduously developed.

The rot within the Church as a structure thus led people to hold that the truth of Christianity was relevant without, or even despite, the actions of the Church itself. This freeing of the message of the poor carpenter from Nazareth, out of necessity from the corruption of the mercenary, military popes, broke the hold, established by Augustine, when he claimed that outside the Church there was no salvation. The Church had to an extraordinary degree, lost the right in the public mind to be the Body of Christ.

This reaction against the Church led to the development of the Inquisition. This body, charged with maintaining that salvation lay only within the Church, used all means possible either to keep people within the Church or to have them killed if they persisted in refusing to be confined by it. This era also saw the rise of witch hunts. Very few witch hunts took place before the 1480s. Thereafter, with the publication of the inquisitors' handbook *Malleus Maleficarum* ('Hammer of the Witches'), witch-hunting became a powerful weapon in the hands of those wishing to instil obedience and fear into increasingly free-thinking and agitating societies. Witch hunts were also, of course, a powerful weapon against women and against the whole store of wisdom and medicinal knowledge which the 'wise women' had traditionally held. It is interesting to note that with the rise of the medical sciences as a respectable and developing sphere of influence and knowledge, the profession became totally male-dominated and not only was the wisdom of the wise women, midwives etc. scorned but they were also persecuted.

The sixteenth century was probably the most dramatic century of Christianity to date. During this period, Christianity began to spread out across the world. Cultures and lands which had never been reached by the gospel were now contacted. Large sections of coastal Africa, North and South America and the wilds of Siberia were beginning to be evangelized. Western Christianity made its first appearance in lands which either had only remnant Eastern churches or where those churches had totally died out, such as India, south-east Asia, China and Japan. The fact that most if not all of this growth went hand in hand with colonialism or mercantile adventures meant that the gospel became almost inextricably linked to Western power, science, thought and money, so much so that any other forms of Christianity – such as the Thomarist churches of India which had existed there for over 1300 years

– were treated as aberrations not worthy of consideration.

THE REFORMATION

The sixteenth century is of course also the century of the Reformation. Beginning in Germany when the former monk Martin Luther nailed his ninety-six complaints against the Church to the cathedral door in Wittenberg in 1517, by the end of the century the Roman Catholic church had lost almost all of northern Europe to the Protestant churches.

The roots of the Reformation are deep and complex. The corruption of the Church, the rise of new understandings from the Renaissance, the restoration of respect for humanity, the new discoveries in science and encounters with new cultures and the struggles for national identity and control by both kings and parliaments, all contributed to this movement and also contributed to its fragmentation into such diverse forms.

The original impulse of the first reformers, such as Martin Luther, was reform of the Church. This they did by attacking those aspects of it which were most caught up in corruption. However, the Church seemed unable to differentiate between attacks on its corruptions and attacks upon its role. Increasingly the reformers found themselves taking positions over the priesthood or the sacraments which placed them outside the definitions of the true faith defined by the Catholic church. It is true to say that the reformers, the founders of the initial Protestant churches did not jump but were pushed out of the fold of the Catholic church.

Had it not been for the secular forces of rising nation states, the free thinking of the Renaissance and the burgeoning of the middle classes in trade, it is likely that the followers of Martin Luther *et al.* would have disappeared as just another heretical sect. That they did not was a sign of the power of these new forces and of the loss of confidence of many ordinary people in the face of the corruption of the Church.

The core of the Protestant revolution was that it elevated the ordinary lay person to a position where they could communicate directly with God and have a proper function within the church. At the same time, the revolution relaxed the social and economic teachings of the faith in order to enable trade and exploitation to develop. In a sense, the Protestant revolution theologically legitimized the development of much of Europe into a sixteenth century version of a free-enterprise zone. It also tried to build the City of God on earth, in ways that varied from the strict Calvinism of Geneva where John Calvin ruled as a theocrat, to the polygamy of the Kingdom of God in Munster of John of Leyden.

In many ways the Protestant revolution opened the door to the rise of democratic ideas. By stating that all were equal before God and by stressing the right of everyone to read the Bible in their own tongue and to be allowed to interpret the Bible according to their conscience (though this was more honoured in the breach than in the observance), the revolution stressed the rights of the individual. The rise of individualism was so fast and so great that it took over as one of the main driving forces. Consider that in 1500 the West had one church yet by the end of the century there were hundreds of churches and sects, and one can see what a break with the monolithic structures of the past the Protestant revolution was.

While there was a strong radical political dimension to the Protestants, this was not the mainstream, and it was often violently opposed by the other Protestant groups. The new churches and sects were too dependent on the wealth and power of their sponsors to be able to side with the poor. Critics of Christianity's influence on the rise of capitalism point to the fact that John Calvin, who ruled the city of Geneva as a holy city from 1555 to his death in 1564, legitimized usury in business. Before Calvin, the church had forbidden usury, a policy which was strictly enforced until the twelfth century, but which had gradually weakened. But it was Calvin, responding to his main support base, who legitimized interest and thus made possible one of the foundations of capitalism.

Let us look briefly at three very different models of the church which arose from the Protestant revolution and of their theologies, before we look at the response of Catholicism.

These three each influenced millions of people and their teachings are still amongst the most powerful forces in Western Christianity and Western society today.

Lutheranism

The first model is Lutheranism. Many countries became Lutheran because their rulers wished to achieve independence from Rome and control over the wealth and power of their national church. Lutheranism takes its basic teachings from the books of Luther such as his *Catechism* (1529), and from gatherings and their resulting pronouncements such as the *Confessions of Augsburg* (1530). They are collected in the *Book of Concord* which was published in 1580.

Unlike the Roman Catholic and Eastern churches, which see the Bible, and the teachings of the fathers and the great ecumenical councils as being partners in developing the Christian faith, Lutheranism sees the Bible as the sole authority. All other writings, such as the creeds or the fathers, are to be judged in the light of the Bible – hence the central importance to the Reformation in having the Bible available in the native languages of the people.

The core teaching of Lutheranism seems to be a return to the negative understanding of humanity of Augustine. Lutheranism teaches that salvation comes about solely through the faith one places in God, what is known as justification by faith alone. No good works can help. It is only the love of God which is capable of rescuing a sinner. Nothing can be done, except to express faith in this love. At times this teaching has led to a kind of fatalism, at other times to a tremendous stress on conversion. Yet the vast majority of Lutheranism has actually functioned on a combination of this model with elements of a more Pelagian sense of the worth and significance of good works and good living.

Lutheranism also taught that the Church must not interfere in the State and vice versa, while also teaching that the State was to be obeyed. This separation of Church and State, combined with the idea of a state church – which is what Lutheranism is in parts of Germany and Scandinavia – resolved the old Church/State tension along new lines. Loyalty to the State was part and parcel of being a Lutheran. But the State must not interfere with the Church. Indeed, some of the Lutherans who opposed Hitler before the Second World War did so not so much because of his treatment of the Jews and others, but because he interfered with the Church.

Anglicanism

The second model is that of the Anglican church, and to some extent the Swedish church. Here there was no revolution. The old Roman Catholic church was simply turned into a state church, with virtually all the structures and many of the teachings of the Roman Catholic church in place, but reformed. It stresses openness, within certain limits, and continuity, whereas many Protestant churches celebrated their break with the past. The theology of this model is gradualist and absorbent rather than systematic and dogmatic. This is seen by many as both a strength and a weakness!

Calvinism

The third model is the one which has most profoundly changed the nature of Christianity, and which has lasting effects to this day. This is the model of the Protestant churches which broke with the past, and which saw only those who did the same as being true Christians. The leading lights in these churches tend to be John Calvin or interpreters of his teachings. It is therefore important to look briefly at these teachings.

Calvin's ideas are set out in his *Institutes*. He agreed with Luther that the Bible was the sole authority for Christians. He also agreed that salvation came only by faith, not by works.

Calvin taught that before the fall, humanity was capable of exercising true free will; we could act rightly or wrongly. After the fall, humanity became incapable of ever doing a good deed. All our actions are tainted by sin and are therefore wrong. Thus all humanity is evil and it is only faith that can offer us any hope of eternal life – there is nothing we can do to achieve it. Calvin lifted the concerns of the kingdom right off this physical world and into the next in no uncertain terms. This life is irreversibly bad. It is only when we are with God in heaven that we can have any sort of 'good' life.

This then led Calvin to a problem. His model of human nature made it necessary to have a God who did not exercise emotion, act in love or bend from a strict sense of justice. God had to be removed from the vagaries of anything which smacked of indecision or that threatened the rule of law. So who could be saved by such a distant and severe God? Calvin's answer was ingenious. He taught that before any person was ever created, before even creation itself began, God had already decided which people would be saved and which damned to eternal hell. This notion of predestination is the hallmark of Calvinism. The role of Jesus was strictly limited to helping those already chosen by God before time began, to be saved. Christ has no role or contribution to make to the vast majority of the world which was born damned and will die damned. Calvin could not reconcile a God of love and compassion with a God of justice and law. Thus he sacrificed the God of love on the altar of law. I am often accused of being tough on Calvin. Frankly, I find his theology so abhorrent and so unchristian that I make no apologies for taking such a negative stance.

It is important to stress here that many of the attitudes within Christianity that modern-day critics attack arise from Calvin's teachings and from the ways in which these teachings – about an elect group, saved and thus able to do pretty much what they want – have been interpreted. To label Christianity, or even all forms of Protestantism, as responsible for the rise of capitalism is wrong. To lay the blame at the door of Calvinism is in part true. Likewise, the extreme, utilitarian ethos about the rest of creation does not come from Christianity, but from a vision of the world in which only a tiny group of the elect have any hope or meaning in their lives.

By the end of the sixteenth century, the main structures of religious thought which were to dominate Europe to our own day had been formed. Not only was Protestant thought set out in its three forms as above and in myriads of mutations and diverse forms springing from and at times rebelling against these three, but the Roman Catholic church had launched the Counter-reformation. In what must count as the most enormous, systematic and successful restructuring and reform ever undertaken by such a body, the Roman Catholic church had purged itself of many of the abuses which had led to the Reformation. It had redefined its theology and had breathed new life into the religious orders, with an unprecedented rise of new orders during the century. Indeed, it is worth pointing out that with a few exceptions, the missionary work which had now reached all the way round the world was undertaken at this time by Roman Catholics (and Russian Orthodox in the north). The Protestant missionary movement came later, or was part of migration rather than explicit mission to other lands.

SECULARISM AND MISSION

The period from the beginning of the seventeenth century to our own day is a story of the development of these strands within Western Christianity as well as the rise, in Europe, of a culture which saw itself as being able to function increasingly well without the ties or justification of religion. Taking Aristotle's model of reason and faith, Aquinas had taught that theology – faith – was the ultimate decider, with the Church as the vehicle which articulated it. Theology was, it was said, the queen of the sciences. By the nineteenth century, this model had been turned on its head. Reason and its sister, science, had come to be the yardstick by which life and even faith were measured. The rise of the scientific, reductionist world view was in part a reaction to the competing cosmologies and dogmas of the churches which had plunged Europe into war after bloody war through much of the sixteenth, seventeenth and early eighteenth centuries. Faith had to a great extent failed on the public scene and had been relegated increasingly to the private world. Reason had come to be the ruling force for most societies by the mid-nineteenth century, leading to that final act of defiance against the rule of the Church over knowledge, the takeover of church schools by the secular state.

While this was happening in Europe itself, the continent sent overseas the largest numbers of missionaries ever recorded. While western and northern Europe – the old heartland of post fifteenth-century Christianity – became increasingly secular in its formal structures, Christianity, often taken abroad by people from these same societies, took root in more cultures and countries than ever before. In many cases, the kind of Christianity which was exported was the sort of individual, quietist (that is to say, emphasizing prayer and minimizing action and responsibility) religion which emerged from the Protestant revolution with its emphasis on the individual and the right to do well materially.

The impact of this new faith on the enslaved, colonialized peoples of Africa, Asia and Latin America was very varied. Some, like the Hindus of India or the Buddhists of Thailand, held firm to their older faiths. Others adopted parts of Christianity and formed new religious groups. The Cao Cao of Vietnam and the many new religious movements of Africa are examples of this. In other places, the enslaved and oppressed discovered that the God of the Bible had a preference for the poor and oppressed. They began to see that the Exodus story was a story about themselves. Drawing on a deeper understanding of the social gospel of Christianity than the average missionary had, they took Luke 4 to heart and in the name of the Christ and God of their masters, demanded freedom and equal rights. The African slaves saw the model of Exodus as the story of their own struggle against the modern-day Egyptians, the Europeans and white Americans. The oppressed masses of south China under the foreign dynasty of the Manchus (who were from Mongolia) saw in the gospel a message of brotherly love and communal life which initially inspired the Taiping Rebellion. Started in 1844 by a visionary who claimed to be Jesus' younger brother, it spread throughout Southern China in the

1850s and nearly toppled the Ching dynasty. It was based upon Christian, socialist and revolutionary notions. This rebellion soon lost its way theologically, and not long afterwards ideologically as well, but it was the greatest peasant revolution in history, lasting over twenty years, leading to the deaths of an estimated twenty million, and affecting hundreds of millions of people. In our own days, the struggle for liberation and political freedom in the colonial empires of the Western nations has often arisen from Christians leading the fight.

LIBERALISM, COMMUNISM AND REFORM

In the West, the crisis of purpose and meaning created by the privatization of religion has given rise to the liberal tradition. This is marked by the development of historical and literary criticism of the Bible. Ironically, this way of criticizing the Bible has emerged primarily from those very Protestant societies where the Bible was held to be the absolute authority. From a position of such absolute authority, most such societies have shifted to the legitimization of doubt.

While the Protestant world has been splitting into yet more and more fragments, the Catholic world has undergone a second reformation with the Vatican Council of the 1960s. Here, many of the reforms sought by the Protestants in the sixteenth century have come to pass. The Catholic church is not the church it was in the 1950s and its changes have unsettled many whilst offering new hope to many more.

The Orthodox churches have been through the fire. They have never had a reformation and could not do so, for the teachings are fixed. But the experience of Communism and the breakdown of the old Church/State model has left them with a mass of new experiences to incorporate into their understanding of faith. With the rise of nationalism, the freedom from atheist ideology and the stark social and economic mess left by dictatorships and Communism, Orthodoxy is having both to recreate its spiritual life and to reinterpret the world it is now allowed to be a part of – a world which is radically different from the one it inhabited so comfortably prior to 1917 in Russia and 1939 in Eastern Europe.

I must confess that I find the present time very exciting as a Christian. The new developments and ideas stirring within the churches and the redefinitions of older traditions and teachings are unparalleled since the sixteenth and seventeenth centuries – indeed it is more dramatic even than in those days. We are telling new or renewed stories and rediscovering stories of the faith which we could not have heard about just a few decades ago, and we are being taught, often painfully, which stories we should now abandon. But what directions are these various movements, with their incredible histories, taking? What is happening to Christianity today and where do the main streams within it seem to be going? For those of us coming from the Western Christian world, where can we draw inspiration for the way to change, and a sense that radical alternative ways of telling the stories of Christianity are both legitimate and true?

To answer this, I want to begin looking at two stories which are rarely if ever heard today. They are important not only because they show how very different Christianity has been, but because they also address issues which are now once again forcefully on the agenda of the faith. We cannot live these stories again, but we can learn from them and see how very, very different Christianity could be, and yet still be faithful to its Saviour.

3

The Celtic Story of Christianity

I was brought up to think that Christianity began in earnest in Britain when St Augustine of Canterbury began his famous mission to Kent, in AD 597. That was the story all my history books gave me, so who was I to argue?

But Christianity in Britain and Ireland is far older than the time of St Augustine of Canterbury. Here in my home city of Manchester, our museum proudly displays a pottery shard which is inscribed with an acrostic of the Lord's Prayer in Latin which was found in a rubbish tip dated from AD 180. In isolated pockets across Roman Britain, mosaics, chalices and jewellery show that Christianity was a part of the complex profusion of beliefs of the Romano-British people from the second century onwards. At the Council of Arles in AD 314, three British bishops were present and the Christians of Britain are referred to by second-century writers such as Origen.

It would appear that much of this Christianity perished along with the Roman way of life after Britain was abandoned by Rome in the first decades of the fifth century. But not all Christianity died out. Nor was all of it associated with the Roman Empire. In Ireland, never occupied by the Romans, and in Scotland, only spasmodically controlled by them, Christianity was developing. But it was, on the whole, unrelated to the Roman Christianity which was the dominant force in the West. Nor did it just draw upon the Graeco-Hebraic traditions to understand the meaning and purpose of creation, of God and of the incarnation. In areas remote from Roman control, a form of Christianity was stirring in the late fourth century which was to create one of the finest Christian civilizations ever, only to be cut short by Rome.

To understand Celtic Christianity, it is necessary to look at the Celts and at the religious traditions which they brought into Christianity.

WHO WERE THE CELTS?

The term Celt is a difficult one to define. It has been used to describe a wide range of groups, probably with an original homeland in the areas of the Russian steppes and the easternmost parts of Europe, some time in the period from the fifth millennium BC. The Greeks and Romans refer to Celts as barbarian invaders who swept down upon the Greek and Roman states. The major encounter between the Celts and the Romans came in Gaul and in parts of Britain. Interestingly enough, there is no extant Roman reference to Celts in Ireland. It would appear that the tribes of Ireland shared many of the religious, cultural and artistic beliefs and styles of the Celts of mainland Europe, but may not have been directly related. In recent years, the term Celt has been used to describe, rather arbitrarily, all those tribal groupings and peoples on the fringes of the Roman world.

Even though we know very little about the Celts, we can see the influence of very clear artistic types across large swathes of Europe. The cultural links between the groups were obviously very strong, and certain motifs occur from the Russian steppes to the western coast of Ireland.

We also know only a little about the religion of these groups. Although various well-intentioned worthies dress up every summer solstice and parade around Stonehenge claiming to be druids, there is very little that we can say for certain about the druids. The present main order is a nineteenth-century romantic invention, whilst the twentieth century has seen the spawning of many imitators.

The Romans stamped out the druids with great ferocity in all the lands that they controlled. They depicted them as blood-thirsty people with a liking for human sacrifices and a whole host of other antisocial habits. The reasons for this are probably more to do with the resistance that the druids organized to Roman rule than to much in the way of historical accuracy. Though Julius Caesar speaks of their barbarity, he also acknowledges that they were highly respected and that their training of young men, and a few women, was of the highest order. But ultimately, they were a threat to the Roman Empire in a way in which other religions were not, with two notable exceptions – Judaism, which Rome sought to destroy when the Jewish revolt of AD 66–70 erupted, and of course Christianity. This link, the link of subversion to the oppressor state, is an important hint at the interaction between these three faiths.

The druids were a caste of priestly wise men and women, set apart from the rest of the community in order to mediate between heaven and earth, and to act as the counsellors and wise ones of their community. As the word druid is thought to come from a Vedic word *vid*, this hints at an Indo-European origin of the order and its beliefs, and the druids could thus be likened to the brahmins in Vedic, now commonly known as Hindu, society.

We know from Roman writers that the druids were able to read and write Greek and Roman, and that they corresponded with centres of education within the Roman Empire. The major colleges were in Britain, until the Romans came, with a massive cultic and educational centre on the Isle of Anglesey, just off the coast of Wales. Here, students underwent twenty years of study before graduating. Sadly we know next to nothing about what they studied or about what they believed. All that we can gather is taken from hostile reports and from what clearly carried over into Celtic Christianity. At its heart there was the use of magic and of human sacrifices – usually the captured enemy. But alongside this were a folklore and healing skills derived from close study and knowledge of the natural world. The natural world was seen, in true shamanistic style, to be alive and vibrant with the divine. To be in touch with this vibrant life was to be in touch with the gods and to be fed by their energy.

The druids, drawing especially upon the mystic powers of oak trees and groves, used this knowledge to hold both the power of healing and the power of social control. Their distinctive clothing appears to have been white gowns and we know that the sign of a druid initiate was that his hair was shaved across the front from ear to ear. This is the special form of tonsure which the Celtic Christian priests also wore. Magic and the ability to transform yourself into other creatures were also strongly held beliefs in druidic circles. Again, we know this from Celtic Christian legends of how saints such as Patrick escaped the druids who were hunting them. St Patrick's breastplate is the chant by which Patrick evoked the protection of the Trinity and of nature, which, according to legend enabled him to be turned into a deer and thus escape the druids.

The druids are one of the most romanticized groups in Europe. It is therefore necessary to dismiss most of the mental images which we might have picked up over the years. Instead we need to first recognize how little we can be sure of about them, but then acknowledge that they were a powerful priestly caste who exercised magic, sacrifice and healing powers. They were scholarly and had an alphabet when most of the 'barbarian' peoples on the fringes of the Greek and Roman empires had no written language. The rigour of their training and their apparent openness to both men and women is also clear.

THE ORIGINS OF CELTIC CHRISTIANITY

Quite how and when Christianity first reached Ireland is unclear. There is an isolated reference to the date 350 and a visit by a group of Eastern monks from Crete. However, I cannot find any further evidence about this statement. But it is likely that Christianity came to Ireland from two sources. The first is from Britain. In Chapter 1 I mentioned St Ninian and his pioneer monastic community at Whithorn. We know that Ninian's grandfather had been a priest of Christ. Ninian lived in the last quarter of the fourth century and the first quarter of the fifth.

This means that his grandfather was a priest in the early fourth century. The family lived in Galloway or possibly nearer to Carlisle, the great north-western Roman army centre. This was an area which had trading links with Ireland, less than thirty miles away from the tip of Galloway. It is inconceivable that Christians from Britain were not travelling to Ireland and sharing the new faith with their fellow Celts. However, it was not the Christianity of the Western Roman Empire which seems to have had the major impact. Instead, the Christianity which seems to have most shaped Irish Celtic Christianity came from thousands of miles away. It came from the deserts of Egypt via the ancient trading routes of the Mediterranean to Ireland.

If you visit the ancient Celtic high crosses of Monasterboice in Ireland, you will see that at the top of one of them are carved two saints. These saints are none other than St Anthony of the desert and St Paul of Thebes, the earliest recorded Christian hermit and the man whom St Anthony went into the desert to visit.

A tenth-century history records the death of seven Coptic (Monophysite church of Egypt) monks in Ireland. There is no clear date given but it has been assumed that this was in the mid to late fifth century. The fact that Coptic monks were in Ireland in such numbers seems to indicate that there was a fairly regular flow of such monks. It is after all not their presence that is commented upon, but their deaths.

In many parts of Ireland, Wales and Scotland, you can find tiny chapels or the remains of hermitages in the most remote and desolate places. Quite often these places will bear names such as Dysart, Disserth or the like. These words are all corruptions of the word desert. And they were so called because in the Celtic monastic tradition, to go to a remote place for spiritual retreat was to go into the desert. The idea of going to the desert is a direct link back to the Coptic monks.

In the Celtic church of Deerhurst in Gloucestershire, there is a strange-shaped window high up on the west wall. Sharp-pointed, tall and angular, it is unlike anything else in architecture in England at that time. The only known window like it anywhere in the world is in one of the most ancient of the churches of Addis Ababa, Ethiopia, founded by Coptic monks moving south. Moreover, the famous highly patterned pages of the Book of Kells are almost identical to the complex 'carpet' designs in contemporary Byzantine and Coptic manuscripts.

I could go on. The point is that we have substantial evidence that the main expressions and traditions of Celtic Christianity came from the monks of Egypt. This means that they came from monks who were rejecting the affluence and power of he official Christianity of the urban areas, the Christianity of the Roman Empire.

Monasticism spread quickly from Egypt. Within fifty years of St Anthony's death and the writing of the Rule of Pachomius, monasteries could be found in Gaul and in Scotland. Here the notion spread down the Celtic fringe, along the West coast of Britain so that within a short period there were monasteries in Scotland and Wales. From these great centres, Christians travelled to Ireland to help what appears to have been a small and struggling church which the Copts had helped to found.

Some writers claim that the druids, encountering a breed of monks who spent long years in the deserts of Egypt or in the wilds of Wales, who lived communally and who passed on collected wisdom and spoke of attaining a higher spiritual awareness, felt a kinship for them. It is impossible to say whether this is true, for we have no records, other than occasional glimpses and hints in writers such as Origen and later Celtic saints, of the earliest days of monastic, Coptic Christianity in Ireland. What is certain is that some form of druidism was still extant in Ireland, for we hear tales of great magical battles with Christian saints such as Patrick in Ireland and Kentigern in Scotland.

It is difficult to say to what extent the druids merged into the priesthood. What we can see is that elements of druidical worship, gods and practices became part of this extraordinary Christianity and that the Celtic Christians saw themselves as being in a continuum from their druidical past. There was no rejection of their past, except for those powers and practices which they saw as antithetical to the God of love. All the artwork, sacred sites, veneration of holy places such as springs and wells and much of the ritual and magic of their former faith was drawn into the new faith of Christianity. Old gods such as Mannon the deity who guided the dead from this world into the next, became saints, so Mannon was identified as Michael, who in Christian tradition guides and protects the soul before and after death.

SAINTS PATRICK AND BRIGID

The greatest of all the saints of Ireland are Patrick and Brigid. St Patrick is a fascinating figure because he, like Ninian, is of two worlds. Born on the west coast of Britain, he was heir, like Ninian, to a family heritage of Christianity stretching back at least to his grandfather, who was a priest. Patrick was born around 385, some ten years before Ninian founded his monastery. Both appear to have come from the Celtic fringe of the expiring Roman world. Both received their initial faith from a Christian family whose links were with the early church and who had gained little if anything from the formal decrees of Constantinople or Theodosius, giving Christianity recognized and then exclusive status within the Empire. By the time Ninian and Patrick were born, the Empire's influence over the remote west areas of Britain was small.

Patrick was taken captive and sold as a slave to Ireland when he was sixteen years old. Here, for six years, he was put to work, and during this time his spiritual quest deepened and he found great solace in his faith.

Having at last escaped from Ireland, he found his way back to his family. But he dreamt of being called back to Ireland. First however he travelled through Gaul studying and was ordained a priest. In 432 he returned to Ireland and began nearly thirty years of remarkable missionary work, drawing together the small Christian communities and confronting both the kingly and the priestly powers of the Celtic kingdoms of Ireland. It is from Patrick's work that the foundations of a strong and confident Church in Ireland spring. The fusion of this strong missionary trend and the Celtic past gave birth to the kind of Christianity which Ireland in particular came to exemplify.

In the life of Patrick we can begin to see the powerful elements which were to form the foundations of the Celtic Christian mix, like the wonderful hymn, *St Patrick's Breastplate*. I wonder how many Christians singing it in church today realize that it is believed to have been a magical chant, based on druidical chants, and with the power of protecting the chanter? The legend goes further and says that when Patrick and his fellow Christians chanted it as they were being pursued by druids, it enabled them to turn into a herd of deer and thus escape their pursuers.

I know of no other Western Christian saint about whom a similar story can be told. It is in direct line from the druidical, shamanistic past of the Celts. What Patrick symbolizes in this one story is the continuity of the Celtic tradition transformed by the meaning of Christianity. In its rich use of all the elements of creation and by its invocation by the world and of nature, it captures the flavour of what Celtic Christianity brought over from the druidical world and what it incorporated from the Christian world. As a credal statement, it is light years away from the careful, urban Greek philosophy of the creeds drawn up by the Councils of Nicea (325) and Chalcedon (451). Here we have the fusion of the Hebrew God of the Old Testament, the reality of the lived life of Jesus Christ and the religious worship of nature of the druids. All brought together and fused in a powerful trinitarian invocation which is at once praise, proclamation and protection. It is worth quoting in full, for it begins to bring us to that vision of the meaning of being a Christian which Celtic Christianity so uniquely developed.

> I breathe in strength as I stand today:
> Calling on the names of the Trinity,
> Believing in the Threeness –
> Witnessing the Oneness –
> On my way to meet You face to face.
>
> I breathe in strength as I stand today:
> With Christ's birth and baptizing –

With the power of his cross and his dying
With the power of his rising and transfiguration
And the power of his descent for the Judgement of Death.

I breathe in strength as I stand today:
With the hierarchy of the Cherubim —
In the willingness of the angels,
Under the wings of the archangels,
Believing in the resurrection to Life —
With the prayers of the Fathers,
With the prophecies of the prophets,
The preaching of the apostles,
The tales of true confession,
The grace of holy women,
And the acts of true men.

I breathe in strength as I stand today:
With the clear blue of Heaven —
The great light of the sun
And the mystery of the moon;
In the blaze of fire —
The flashing of lightning —
In the speed of the wind,
In the depths of Ocean
In the rootedness of earth
And the reality of rock.

I breathe in strength as I stand today:
With the love of God to guide me —
His strength to overlight me,
His wisdom to sustain me,
His eye to see for me
His ear to listen through me
His Word to utter me
His hand to hold me
His road to reach before me —
His shield to protect me,
His host to save me
From the subtlety of demons,
The temptations of evil,
The lusts of my nature
And from those who wish me dead

From far away, and near
Alone, and in the multitude.

And I summon today between us all this
Against everything that threatens my innermost heart:
The tongues of false prophets –
The darkness of gods and goddesses,
The false blessing of heretics,
The icons of idolatry,
The spells of smiths and witchy priests,
And every force that muddies a man's being.

Christ be my strength today
Against poisoning, burning,
Drowning and maiming –
So that I can be as I truly am.

Christ be with me, in front of me, behind me
Christ inside me, under me and over me
Christ to my right, and left, where I lie
Christ where I sit and Christ as I rise
Christ in the heart of everyone who thinks of me,
Christ in the mouth of everyone who speaks of me,
Christ in the eyes of all who see me
Christ in every ear that hears me.

I breathe in strength as I stand today:
Calling on Father, Son and Holy Spirit
Believing in the Threeness,
Witnessing the Oneness,
On my way to meet You face to face.

> Version composed by Jay Ramsey for this book

Patrick died in 461, having set the Church in Ireland firmly on the map and having established monastic and educational settlements similar to those on the west coasts of Britain. In his work, he drew together the genius of pre-Christian faith in the divine and nature, in the forces of the spiritual world and the inherent value of this material world.

In his last few years, he baptized and talked to a young girl who was eight or so when he died. Her name was Brigid and after St Patrick she is accounted the most important saint of Ireland. Her true life is very hard to uncover in the wealth of legends and conflicting stories which are told about her. The bare bones which can be discerned already give a hint of the role she has played in bridging the world of pre-Christian Celtic faith and the newly emerging world of Celtic Christianity.

In Celtic mythology, Brigid was the mother of the gods and goddesses. She was also the goddess of childbirth, of the sacred fire and of water. She was patron of the crafts and art as well as of healing powers. So venerated was she that one entire tribe of pre-Roman Britons in the north of England took her name as their tribal name – the Brigantes of the area now covered by Lancashire and Cumbria. The feast of Brigid was at the beginning of February, the time of the traditional start of spring. The feast day of *St* Brigid is February 1st.

St Brigid founded a nunnery and monastery at what is now Kildare. The original name was Cill-Dara meaning the church of the oaks. Here is a direct link to the druids and their worship of oaks. The twin monastery/nunnery was a special feature of Celtic monasticism and it was far from unusual for such joint communities to be ruled by a woman. The restrictions on women playing a major role within the Church and its hierarchy was unknown in Celtic Christianity.

A special feature of the monastery of St Brigid was the sacred or holy fire kept burning there. The ritual of maintaining a fire for decades and centuries was a feature of druidical worship and was associated with sacred oak groves. In the twelfth century, Gerald of Wales, the historian, priest and inveterate traveller, visited the nunnery of St Brigid at Kildare and reports in his *Travels in Ireland* on the fire at the nunnery:

> This they call inextinguishable, not because it could not be extinguished but because the nuns feed it with fuel and so carefully that it has ever continued inextinct from the time of the virgin [Brigid] and not withstanding the great quantity of wood that has been consumed during so long a time, yet the ashes have never accumulated. . . . The fire is surrounded by a circular fence of twigs within which a male enters not, and if one should chance to presume to enter, which was sometimes attempted by giddy persons, he escapes not without enduring punishment. Also, it is

permitted only for women to blow the fire, and for these, not with their own breath, but with bellows or fans.

(*The Celtic Alternative*, by Shirley Toulson, Rider, 1987, p. 71).

The sacred fire of the druids in the grove of oaks has passed without interruption into the holy fire of St Brigid in the church of the oaks.

Brigid is also strongly linked and associated with the Virgin Mary. Perhaps in a romantic attempt to hold together elements of the worship of the pre-Christian goddess Brigid and the historical but legendized Brigid the abbess, there is a charming story told that Brigid was the midwife found by Joseph to help Mary give birth to the Saviour. In having a Brigid fulfil the role of handmaiden to the handmaiden of God, the Celtic church was in effect saying that the old goddess had been a witness to the new Saviour, that there was a continuum of holiness and of the divine and that their pre-Christian past was a worthy forerunner of their Christian present.

I have given these stories of Patrick and Brigid as illustrations of how the Celtic church made sense of and gave meaning to its pre-Christian past and drew this into its Christian identity. This is in marked contrast to the destruction of the ancient cultures and beliefs which, at exactly the same time, Justinian, ruler of the Byzantine Empire, was carrying out in the ancient School of Athens and to the remnants of pagan worship in the east of the old Roman Empire. In Ireland, the transition from druidic to Christian life seems to have flowed with only a few moments of direct confrontation. Having no imperial army, nor being part of a dominant Christian culture, the gospel in Ireland had to make its way by debate, example, lifestyle and truth, and by building upon what it found already there in terms of under-standing the divine. It was taking a very different path from most Roman/Byzantine theology and Christianity of its time.

MONASTICISM, SAINT COLUMBA AND IONA

We now come to the figure of Columba, the foundation of Iona and from there the spread of the Celtic Christian faith across Scotland and northern England.

Celtic Christianity was unique in many ways, but its most distinctive organizational feature was the role of monasteries and monks. In the Roman Empire, and indeed in the east, beyond the Romans, Christianity was largely an urban religion. The desert monks of course stand out as an alternative strand, but it is an alternative, not a mainstream expression of Christianity. Christianity also adopted the Roman notion of areas ruled by a governor, called dioceses in the old Roman administration, and still called dioceses in some Christian churches today.

Celtic Christianity was the reverse. It was a rural faith, for there were no cities in Ireland nor in those parts of Wales and Scotland where the Church established its footholds. It was a Christianity of the wild and remote areas, of islands and rocky crags. The people amongst whom it spread lived in isolated hamlets or large farmsteads, with every so often, a larger encampment where the local chief or king ruled. The older religion of the druids had been based in the forests and woods, though there is evidence to show that the druidical colleges had permanent buildings, not unlike the later monasteries.

The essence of this remote, rural Christianity is captured in many prayers and hyms of the Celtic church. This one is simply known as *The Wish of Manchan of Liath*, and comes from the tenth century.

I wish, ancient and eternal King, to live in a hidden hut in the wilderness.

A narrow blue stream beside it, and a clear pool for washing away my sins by the grace of the Holy Spirit.

A beautiful wood all round, where birds of every kind of voice grow up and find shelter.

Facing southwards to catch the sun, with fertile soil around it suitable for every plant.

And virtuous young men to join me, humble and eager to serve
God.

Twelve young men three fours, four threes, two sixes, six pairs —
willing to do every kind of work.

A lovely church, with a white linen cloth over the altar, a home for
God from heaven.

A Bible surrounded by four candles, one for each of the Gospels.

A special hut in which to gather for meals, talking cheerfully as we
eat, without sarcasm, without boasting, without any evil words.

Hens laying eggs for us to eat, leeks growing near the stream,
salmon and trout to catch and bees providing honey.

Enough food and clothing given by our Heavenly King, and
enough time to sit and pray to him.

(*Celtic Fire* by Robert van de Weyer, DLT, 1990, p. 92)

In this sketch of the ideal monastic group, all the salient features
are found of the Celtic monastery. Simple huts and tasks; a
farming and gathering existence and worship. The monasteries,
in lieu of any towns or cities, came to be the centres of power
and authority for the Celtic church. There were of course
bishops; the first recorded one was sent by Pope Celestine
(422–432), St Palladius, who did not have great success, being
an avid Roman and opposed to the Celtic monk Pelagius. But
the bishops were almost always subservient in all practical
matters to the great abbots and abbesses. The stories of St
Brigid tell of her selecting the bishop for her area, one Conleath,
with whom she got on very well.

This community-based leadership, the educational role, the
sponsorship and execution of artistic work and the meditational
lifestyle of these monastic centres, drew upon both Christian
and, as far as we can see, druidical models, informed by the
spirituality of the Egyptian deserts. The mixture produced the
first genuinely rural and nature-based Christianity in the world.
It is this which we celebrate today when we look into the
Christian past to discover whether Christianity is irredeemably
a hierarchical, imperialist and urban phenomenon.

The spread of this form of Christianity from Ireland to Scotland and then down into northern England and further afield was entirely dependent on monasticism. This brings us to Columba and the role of Iona.

St Columba was born around 521 and came from a wealthy and powerful Irish family. He was trained in the monastic tradition and established various churches and monasteries. He was a fiery man, who fused the drive and vigour of the Celts with the passion for the cross of the Christians. In 563 he left Ireland. The reasons are not clear, but it seems likely that he withdrew because of his involvement in a bloody battle between different tribes. Whatever the reason, he left and found himself on the island of Iona. Here he founded what was to become the foremost missionary monastery in the Celtic world. From Iona, Columba travelled extensively in Scotland, performing miracles such as driving away a monster from the river Ness, the earliest reference in writing to the fabled Loch Ness Monster. Through his efforts, the Picts of Scotland were gradually converted, starting with one of the tribal kings, Brude. In 574, the new King of Argyll, Aidan, came to Columba to be consecrated as king.

St Aidan, a monk at Iona, was sent in 635 in response to a request by Oswald the King of Northumbria to bring the gospel to the people of northern England. Oswald gave Aidan the island of Lindisfarne as a base and here a great monastic centre equal to Iona arose. Aidan was deeply loved for the simplicity of his lifestyle, the power of his teachings and the compassion of his actions. Through his missionary work, Christianity took firm root and began to spread down the east coast of England.

Before looking at the sudden and, to many people, tragic break-up of this Celtic church by the Roman church, let us examine the distinctive theology and practice which marks the Celtic church out from its larger and more powerful brother.

THE WORLD OF THE CELTIC CHRISTIANS

Recently I have been reading a great deal of Celtic prayer and writings. I have been impressed by the directness and beauty of so much of these writings. It is as if they saw the world through eyes which divined the godly within all and saw all as godly. In my reading, I allowed my intellect to be excited. Here was an expression of Christianity which had nothing of the Protestant guilt complex about enjoyment, nor the master/manager language of the Roman Catholic church with regard to nature. But my excitement was largely the intellectual excitement of finding a theology which expressed many of my feelings about our role in nature. Then I set off from my office one evening to cycle home.

I have cycled that route, through urban Manchester, hundreds of times. That evening, as the light faded I found myself looking at it through the eyes of the Celtic Christian prayers. I don't know if I can convey in words what happened. But suddenly I saw a world I had never seen before. It was as if through the prayers my awareness and sensitivity to all around me had been heightened to an extraordinary degree. The road I take from the office suddenly had trees and bushes I had never seen before. The pattern of the landscape was like a picture laid out for me. I found myself caught up in the space of the skies above and the movement of the rain clouds. It was a most remarkable experience of heightened awareness. It was at that moment that I really came to understand what the Celtic Christians were talking about. One of my favourite prayers is the psalm of St Columba, who used to leave Iona and retreat to a remote island for prayer. Thank God he knew nothing of the growing fear of nature and the dislike of the material world which was beginning to eat into Roman Christianity.

> Delightful I think it to be in the bosom of an isle, on the peak of a rock, that I might often see there the calm of the sea.

> That I might see its heavy waves over the glittering ocean, as they chant a melody to their Father on their eternal course.

That I might see its smooth strand of clear headlands, no gloomy thing; that I might hear the voice of the wondrous birds, a joyful tune.

That I might hear the sound of the shallow waves against the rocks; that I might hear the cry by the graveyard, the noise of the sea.

That I might see its splendid flocks of birds over the fullwatered ocean; that I might see its mighty whales, greatest of wonders.

That I might see its ebb and its flood-tide in their flow; that this might be my name, a secret I tell, 'He who turned his back on Ireland.'

That contrition of heart should come upon me as I watch it; that I might bewail my many sins, difficult to declare.

That I might bless the Lord who has power over all, Heaven with its pure host of angels, earth, ebb, flood-tide.

That I might pore on one of my books, good for my soul; a while kneeling for beloved Heaven, a while at psalms.

A while gathering dulse from the rocks, a while fishing, a while giving food to the poor, a while in my cell.

A while meditating upon the Kingdom of Heaven, holy is the redemption; a while at labour not too heavy; it would be delightful!

(Translation from *A Celtic Miscellany* by Kenneth Hurlstone Jackson, Penguin, 1951, pp. 279–80).

This sense of sheer delight in all that is of God is perhaps one of the most refreshing things about Celtic Christianity. There is none of the rejection of the natural world which so scarred Roman Christianity as it sought to defeat the pagan faiths of Europe. In the Celtic tradition, the natural world was sacred not in its own right, but because it was made and loved by God. It is this sense of God in and through all things which so forcefully confronts the reader in the prayers and teachings of the Celtic church. There is no hesitancy about the goodness of this world, no attempt to see it as in some way a flawed or imperfect world in the semi-gnostic and Manichaean way that much traditional

Christianity sees it. In a world where we are seeking to understand the divine and the natural in order to prevent ourselves committing the blasphemy of destroying most of the natural world, the Celtic tradition speaks vividly across the centuries. Listen to the creed or catechism which later Celtic tradition ascribed to St Ninain:

Question: What is best in this world?
Answer: To do the will of our Maker.

Question: What is his will?
Answer: That we should live according to the laws of his creation.

Question: How do we know these laws?
Answer: By study – studying the Scriptures with devotion.
Question: What tool has our Maker provided for this study?
Answer: The intellect, which can probe everything.

Question: What is the fruit of study?
Answer: To perceive the eternal Word of God reflected in every plant and insect, every bird and animal and every man and women.

(*Celtic Fire*, by Robert van de Weyer, DLT, 1990, p. 65)

In *The Black Book of Carmarthen*, a treasured, ancient Welsh book, the following poem meditates upon this ability to know God through perceiving that he is all creation:

> I am the wind that breathes upon the sea,
> I am the wave on the ocean,
> I am the murmur of leaves rustling,
> I am the rays of the sun,
> I am the beam of the moon and stars,
> I am the power of trees growing,
> I am the bud breaking into blossom,
> I am the movement of the salmon swimming,
> I am the courage of the wild boar fighting,
> I am the speed of the stag running,
> I am the strength of the ox pulling the plough,
> I am the size of the mighty oak,
> And I am the thoughts of all people,
> Who praise my beauty and grace.

It is important to note that Celtic Christianity did not believe that God was identical with creation. God is always greater than creation. This is made clear in the great Celtic Psalter which opens thus

> My dear King, my own King, without pride, without sin, you created the whole world, eternal, victorious King.

> King above the elements, King above the sun, King beneath the ocean, King of the north and south, the east and west, against you no enemy can prevail.

> King of the Mysteries, you existed before the elements, before the sun was set in the sky, before the waters covered the ocean floor; beautiful king, you are without beginning and without end . . .

Celtic Christianity was able to hold in tension both the immanence and the transcendence of God. God is in and through all things and is above and below all things. Nothing is incapable of speaking of God and all are filled with the potential of God – not least, us. To deny the godliness of anything, even in the name of religion, is to go against that which God really wanted – for you to enjoy and celebrate life in all its fullness.

This emphasis on the legitimacy of enjoying all that is beautiful in creation is brought out in the following tale of a rather over-zealous and obviously rather difficult young monk, Moling, who lived around the middle of the seventh century in Ireland. One day, Moling was in the church of the monastery and his brothers were eating their supper in the refectory. A young man appeared in the refectory carrying a harp. He asked if he might play for the monks, who readily agreed. When he had played for them they shared their food with him.

During the meal, the young man asked which of them was the famous Moling whose austerity was renowned. The brothers replied that Moling was in church for he fasted on three days of the week rather than the usual one. Finishing his meal the young man picked up his harp and went to the church. The other monks shook their heads, knowing that Moling would never allow himself to listen to music while he prayed. Such enjoyment was not for him.

The young man went into the church to find Moling kneeling in prayer. Taking his harp, he started to play, at which Moling, without appearing to acknowledge his presence, took two balls of wax from his pocket and stuffed them into his ears.

The young man simply continued to play, with a smile upon his face the whole time. To Moling's astonishment, the wax began to melt. Nothing he did would stop it dissolving. At just this moment the young man picked up a sharp stone and began to scrape it across the strings, producing a terrible screeching noise. As the noise continued, Moling found it more and more unbearable until suddenly the young man began to play sweetly again. As the beautiful music flowed from the harp again, Moling found it soothed him and transported him with delight.

When the young man finished, Moling asked him, 'Are you a devil sent to tempt me or an angel sent to bless me?'

The young man replied, 'You must make your own judgement. When I scraped the harp with the stone, it was like the noise of the devil. When I played it with my fingers it sounded like an angel. Music, like food and drink, can be the agent of the devil or a source of goodness.'

The young man then left leaving Moling to his thoughts. But from that day on Moling welcomed all musicians to the monastery. He gave up his austere pattern of fasting and just fasted when everyone else did. And his brother monks could not help noticing from that day on, Moling was more gentle and kind, and that he even developed a sense of humour!

Throughout Celtic Christianity this sense of the celebration of life in all its fullness is to be found. The art and the poetry show this, as do the stories of the holy men and women. This was an expression of Christianity which took the pleasures and beauty of the world as something to sing and dance about. It is therefore interesting to note how sin and repentance feature in the faith.

The idea that within the grace and bounty of God humanity is often at odds and therefore needs forgiveness and reconciliation is clearly stated in the Celtic prayers. But a distinctive feature of Celtic belief was that in struggling with your own journey in faith, you travelled with a soul friend which was called an *anamchara*. This person would guide you in your meditations and actions, acting as a spiritual director. The *anamchara* was the wise one who had painfully trodden the way before you and who was there to steady and guide you when necessary. Such a person had his or her own *anamchara* and thus the individual was in a long line, a network of those seeking to follow Christ. There is a feeling that the individual was caught up in a great company of saints and angels and that they were journeying onwards, walking side by side with one who knew the way. Equally important, this sense of being in communion with one another and with God was set within a framework of images of God which broadened and deepened the normal terms derived from the Church and the Bible alone. The sixth-century prayer attributed to St Ciaran captures this sense.

O Father, O Son, O Holy Spirit,
Forgive me my sins.
O only begotten Son of the heavenly Father,
Forgive, O one God, O true God, O chief God,
O God of one substance, O God only mighty, in three persons,
  truly pitiful,
Forgive.

O God above all gods, O Kings above all kings, O Man above
  men,
Forgive.
O World above worlds, O Power above powers, O love above
  loves,
O Cause above causes, O Fortress above fortresses,
O Angel above angels,
Forgive.

Archdeacon of heaven and earth,
Forgive. O High Priest of all creation,
O Archbishop of the seven heavens,
Forgive. O first Priest, O chief Priest,
O true Priest, O true Physician, O true Prophet, O true Friend,
Forgive.

O only Sustainer of the threefold mansion, O only Life of all
created things,
O only Light of the seven heavens,
Forgive. O subject of the Scriptures' meditation,
O Object of the chief prophets' search, O Father of true life,
O voice of the people,
Forgive.

(Quoted in *A World Made Whole*, by Esther de Waal, Fount, 1991,
pp. 104–5).

THE ASCETIC TRADITION

The ascetic tradition within Celtic Christianity was also strong.
It is important to recall the tremendous life-affirming dimensions of Celtic Christianity and its love of and revelling in the
beauties of nature, for otherwise some aspects of Celtic Christian asceticism can seem narrow. The story of Moling shows
how some monks took penitence too far and were in effect
reprimanded by angels. There is also a sense that once the Celtic
church lost its own freedom, it diverted its energies into leading
a more demanding and ascetical lifestyle than any other branch
of the Western church.

In Celtic Christianity there were three forms of martyrdom,
in the sense not just of physical death, but of the death of all
that prevents the soul from attaining to God. There was first of
course the actual martyrdom of being killed for your faith. This
was known as red martyrdom. Then there was white martyrdom. This was when a Christian left all that he or she loved and
was familiar with, and set off to wander the world, preaching
the gospel. Columba, leaving his beloved Ireland was one such.
The gospel was taken throughout Scotland, northern England,
Wales and Brittany by such people. Finally there was green
martyrdom, when the Christian lived in simplicity and humility,
fasting and praying.

Salvation for the Celtic Christian was also to be a partaker in
something much bigger and more wonderful than just individual freedom or salvation. Christ was the greatest symbol of
liberation and freedom. In Celtic prayers, a litany of saving

actions is given, from Noah and Lot to the great saints of Ireland. God has constantly been at work, plucking people from destruction – either of their own making or resulting from the actions of others. The sense in many of the prayers is of humanity gallantly struggling, but being beset with troubles often beyond their ken. At this moment of crisis, Christ or one of the saints appears to take the load and to free the Christian from trouble, not in order that they should then never be in trouble again, but in order to reassure them that whenever they are in trouble, Christ is beside them.

It is a powerful vision, founded upon the promise of Christ made, according to St Matthew, at the very moment when he ascended to heaven – 'Know that I am with you, even until the end of time.' This sense of being protected, as in the breastplate prayer of Patrick, is totally trinitarian in formula. There is no sense in Celtic Christianity of Jesus being set against or having to answer to the Father. There is no hint of a cosmic struggle which is only resolved through the sacrifice of Christ. Rather, there is a sense of the trinity being three equal aspects of God, working in perfect harmony to bring goodness, love and joy to the earth and to humanity. It is refreshing to find the trinity thus expressed when so much of Christianity has spoken in such a way as to make the Father remote from the Son, if not at times, actually saying that the Son had to oppose the Father. The following prayers from the great collection of Celtic prayers and writings, the *Carmina Gadelica* convey this.

The compassing of God and His right hand
Be upon my form and upon my frame;
The compassing of the High King and the grace of the Trinity
Be upon me abiding ever eternally,
Be upon me abiding ever eternally.

May the compassing of the Three shield me in my means,
The compassing of the Three shield me this day,
The compassing of the Three shield me this night,
From hate, from harm, from act, from ill.

Be the eye of God dwelling with you,
The foot of Christ in guidance with you,

The shower of the Holy Spirit pouring on you,
Richly and generously.

The Celtic tradition of Christianity knew evil to be a reality. Celtic Christianity believed in the devil and evil forces, but not in their ability to hold their own with the cross or with the power of the trinity. Nor did they believe that the natural, the material world, was evil or even fallen. The fall seems to have been viewed purely as a human problem, but one which was far from insurmountable. They saw good in human actions as being a way to partially overcome this fall, and do not seem to have held that just being human meant that you were sinful. Instead they exude a powerful sense that God is present in even the most mundane, ordinary and humble things, that nothing should be dismissed as worthless or tainted by sin, but that all should be seen as coming from God. It is this freedom from any hint of Augustine's problems with original sin, this Pelagian sense (don't forget that Pelagius was almost certainly a Christian from Celtic origins) of the potential for good within all people, which makes Celtic Christianity such a change.

THE BREAKING OF THE CHURCH

So what happened to this Christianity? Why did it not become the dominant form of the faith at least in Britain? The answer is that it was broken by Rome.

In 597, Pope Gregory the Great sent Augustine, the prior of a monastery in Rome, to convert the Kentish tribes of southern England and to bring Roman Christianity back to a Roman province which had been effectively cut off for over 150 years. Augustine was successful in that he converted the King of Kent, Ethelbert, whose wife, a Christian, had asked for the mission.

In 603 or thereabout, Augustine travelled to somewhere in the west (rumour has it that it was the site of the later, great Augustinian monastery of Bristol) to meet representatives of the Celtic churches of Wales, Ireland, Scotland and northern England. These bishops and abbots of the Celtic church were far from impressed by Augustine and his claims about the rights and rules of Rome. They refused to acknowledge him as their archbishop and they refused to abandon their own version of Christianity.

But the die had been cast. The Roman mission slowly spread further north and west from the heartland of Augustine's mission area, Kent and London. As it did, it increasingly encountered Celtic churches, such as the one founded by St Cedd at Bradwell on Sea in Essex. The two churches' traditions clashed on many points, but the most serious were the method to be used for fixing the date of Easter and the hierarchy of power within the church itself. The Celtic church had its own method of calculating the date of Easter which closely resembled that used in the Orthodox church. The Roman church was already at loggerheads with the Orthodox church over this.

In terms of authority and theology, the Roman church followed an imperial order, with secular and spiritual power lying with the bishops and everyone else being subservient to them. In the Celtic church, bishops were on a par with and often subservient to, the great abbots and abbesses. Men and women had equal authority as heads of monastic communities, and as with St Brigid, women could be heads of mixed communities of men and women. The spiritual father, the soul friend, was considered more important than any hierarchy and the great saints and hermits held a specially revered place.

Being a monastic church, the Celtic church regarded community as more important than authority. Rome on the other hand, operated in a very different way. Using a model derived from the Empire, it placed authority first. Having become a very wealthy and powerful institution, and seeing the world as fallen, it took upon itself the right to govern all aspects of life and to control the behaviour of its faithful, as well as the right to punish or restrict those who were not Christians. It was an authoritarian model with an individual – the pope – as its head, whilst the Celtic church was communal, with no one person at its head. Rome saw the city of God as something opposed to the physical realities of this world; the Celts knew no city, but celebrated the wonders of God revealed in all aspects of the physical and material world. Rome saw the physical world as fallen and humanity as damned; the Celts saw the world as a wonder and humanity as part of that wonder. Rome saw Christ as having to pay a price for the justice of God and the sin of humanity; the Celts saw Christ within the context of the trinity. Here Christ reigned alongside the Father and the Spirit who in harmony sought to reach out and touch all aspects of life through their own experiences as creator, suffering one and inspirer.

As was to be the case later in English Christianity, the denouement came as a result of the need for marital happiness of a king of England. King Oswy, King of Northumbria, was brought to Christianity through the Celtic saints of Lindisfarne and thus kept the Celtic Easter. His wife, Eanfled, came from the Roman areas of Kent, and had a different date for Easter. As Bede puts it in his *A History of the English Church and People*.

> It is said that the confusion in those days was such that Easter was sometimes kept twice in one year, so that when the king had ended Lent and was keeping Easter, the Queen and her attendants were still fasting and keeping Palm Sunday.
>
> Penguin Classic translation by Leo Sherley-Price, 1955, p. 186)

To resolve this, and I suspect because he wanted to align himself with the rising power of the Roman kingdoms of the south, King Oswy called a synod of the churches in Britain to discuss the issue of the date. It was to turn into a debate about the status of the Celtic church itself. Pressure had already been brought to bear upon the Celtic clergy. Bede records that Oswy's son Alchfrid, who had gone over to the Roman church. had ousted a community of Celtic monks from a new site at Ripon when they had refused to adopt the Roman ways.

The Synod of Whitby

In 664, the bishops, monks and rulers gathered at the remarkable twin monastery for men and women at Whitby, ruled by St Hilda. Here, after prolonged debate, Oswy decided to fall in line with the Roman date for Easter and to purge the church of those who would not. The Celtic church had lost against the powers of Rome. Many of its monks and priests moved away from England and out of the reach of the Roman church. Some decided to abandon their old ways. The Celtic church began to lose control of more and more of its monasteries and holy places as Roman influence spread further and further north and into Wales and Ireland. While Celtic practices lived on in some places for another 200 years or more, the Celtic church suffered a blow at the Synod of Whitby from which it never recovered. How can a communal church fight a hierarchical one which links so effectively with secular powers?

At Whitby, British Christianity lost its original faith and its positive vision of humanity and nature, and was brought firmly within the growing theology of the Roman, Western church which began to impose dogmas where formerly there had been faith. It is not without a certain bitter irony that it was this English, Roman church which not only abandoned the dynamic loving model of the Celtic trinity, but which through Anselm and substitutionary atonement, envisaged the trinity as an angry, unforgiving Father and a sacrificed son!

A sad story now unfolds. Celtic monks were often given a straightforward choice: either conform to Rome or leave your monastic centres. Many left, taking off into the hills and into the remote glens and islands of the north of England and Scotland, the teachings and in particular the prayers of their tradition. In Ireland, the influence of Rome slowly crept up from the south, replacing the old church with new structures, dioceses and episcopal control, which stifled the Celtic monasticism. This, coupled with the crippling effects of the invasions of the Norsemen, damaged the Church greatly, though it continued to send out missionaries to many parts of northern Europe until the eleventh century. Some centres of Celtic Christianity survived for over a hundred years or so – Iona being one such place. Here the tradition was handed on from abbot to abbot. But eventually even these great centres had to conform. The Celtic church in Wales survived longest. It was not until 1203 that all its ancient centres – St David's, St Asaph's, Bangor and Llandaff – surrendered to the authority of the Archbishop of Canterbury and thus to Rome.

Whitby marked the beginning of the end of Celtic Christianity as a great church standing in its own right. From 664 onwards, it was a church in retreat, holding a few areas but losing ground everywhere at the formal and structural level. The victorious Roman church sought to obliterate it, so that it is still possible to go to Dublin today and to be shown the Book of Kells and famous Celtic monastic sites, with no mention of the Celtic church. With the Synod of Whitby, the indigenous church of the Celts was placed firmly outside the pale of conventional Christianity. Its theology as well as its lifestyle was by implication seen as in error, if not actually wrong. The take-over of the monasteries, which began immediately after the Synod of Whitby, was designed to deliver a death blow to the very heart of Celtic Christianity. What took longer to suppress was the art which incorporated with such freedom symbols and deities from the Celtic past and the faith in the triune God. For many people today, it is an encounter with one of these fascinating stone crosses of the Celtic Christians which makes them realize that once there was a form of Christianity in the islands of Great Britain and Ireland which saw the world and the meaning of Christ and the love of God in a very different way.

THE LIVING LEGACY

Celtic Christianity as an ordered, monastic-based expression of faith died out. But the prayers, sayings, stories and insights of the church continued, albeit underground. Over the last hundred years, strands of it have been found well and alive in the Scottish islands, and the refounding of the community at

Iona has done an immense amount to preserve and breathe new life into this most ancient Christianity. In particular, as Christianity has had to look at the detrimental effects of certain aspects of its Western, Roman and Protestant forms – disregard of nature, pessimism about the world and humanity, the rise of the just God and his appeasement – many have found the very different faith of the Celtic church to be a ray of hope; a way of being Christian, I would say even more faithfully Christian, while not having to believe in those life-denying aspects of the Western church at its worst.

Perhaps we need a second Synod of Whitby, at which we can opt for the non-hierarchical, nature-revering, trinity-adoring and all-embracing faith of the Celtic church and we can drop away from us the forms and vestiges, hierarchy and complexes of the Roman/Western church. Perhaps it is time we returned to Whitby and chose again.

I would like to leave this account of the Celtic church by returning to the delight and godliness that it perceived in everyday things, and the good within all around us that offers such hope. The following are two prayers taken from the *Carmina Gadelica*:

> This morning, as I kindle the fire upon my hearth, I pray that the flame of God's love may burn in my heart and the hearts of all I meet today.
>
> I pray that no envy and malice, no hatred or fear, may smother the flame.
> I pray that indifference and apathy, contempt and pride, may not pour like cold water on the fire.
>
> Instead, may the spark of God's love light the love in my heart, that it may burn brightly through the day.
>
> And may I warm those that are lonely, whose hearts are cold and lifeless, so that they all may know the comfort of God's love.

The peace of God, the peace of humanity,
The peace of Columba kindly,
Mary mild, the loving

Christ, king of tenderness,
The peace of Christ, king of tenderness.
Be upon each window, upon each door,
Upon each hole that lets in light,
Upon the four corners of my house,
Upon the four corners of my bed,
Upon the four corners of my bed.

Upon each thing my eye takes in,
Upon each thing my mouth takes in,
Upon my body that is of earth,
And upon my soul that comes from on high,
Upon my body that is of earth,
And upon my soul that comes from on high.

4

The Chinese Nestorian Stories of Christianity

Having just looked at a form of Christianity which developed on the furthest western flanks of the Christian world, I want to take you right across the world to the east, to China, and to one of the most extraordinary stories of the Christian faith.

It will take us into an encounter between Christianity, Buddhism and Taoism which left all three faiths changed and which led to the transformation of the Virgin Mary into a female Buddhist deity now revered across the face of China and Japan. It is the story of the Nestorian church in China, perhaps one of the least-known but potentially most significant forms of Christianity ever, and one whose experience of pluralism contains hints for us as we struggle with Christianity and diversity.

THE NESTORIAN CHURCH

The roots of the great Nestorian Church of the East lie, in common with many other more orthodox churches of the East, in Antioch. Here Christianity, still a mainly Jewish faith, first had its major contact with Gentiles. Here also, so the Acts of the Apostles says, the followers of Jesus were first called Christians (Acts 11–26). From Antioch, trade routes led off into the East, to Syria, Arabia, Persia and beyond. Down these trade routes went the new faith. It was very successful. In part this was due to the presence of very large, long-established Jewish communities

– first deposited there after the fall of Jerusalem to the Babylonians in 587 BC. These communities had spread the notions of Judaism quite widely, and there were local kings who had converted to Judaism in areas such as present-day Mosul in the Kurdish area of Iraq.

So successful was this Christian mission, that well over a hundred years before Constantine converted, and a hundred years before Armenia did so, the city state of Edessa (modern-day Urfa in southern Turkey) had made Christianity its formal faith.

When Constantine converted, the Eastern church suffered great persecution by the Persian dynasty of the Sassanians. The Sassanians saw their great historic enemy become Christian and they thus began to consider the growing community of Christians in their own empire as a threat. Spurred on by the Zoroastrian priests – the exponents of the formal religion of the Persian Empire – the shahs launched a wave of attacks on the Church. This had the effect of breaking the ties between the churches of the East in the Roman and Persian areas. It also made the Christians in Persia anxious to stress that they were not a fifth column and that they were quite capable of being both loyal citizens and Christians, and to look for clear ways of showing that they did not agree with or support the imperial policies of the Byzantine church. For most of the fourth century, however, the Persian church suffered under a grievous persecution.

In 410, after pressure was brought to bear by Constantinople, the Shah, Yazdegard I, was persuaded to meet the Church to discuss a workable resolution of the situation. A council was called at Seleucia, the originally Greek city founded opposite the more ancient Ctesiphon, the capital of the empire. Here the Church and the dynasty worked out a *modus vivendi* which was later to be adopted by the Muslims, and became the very system under which the Church in Constantinople and the rest of the Eastern Roman Empire was to operate. The system established the Church as a self-governing body, responsible for the civic behaviour of its faithful in relation to the secular authorities. The Council of Seleucia gave it the right to govern itself and its people by a number of laws and to have a degree of

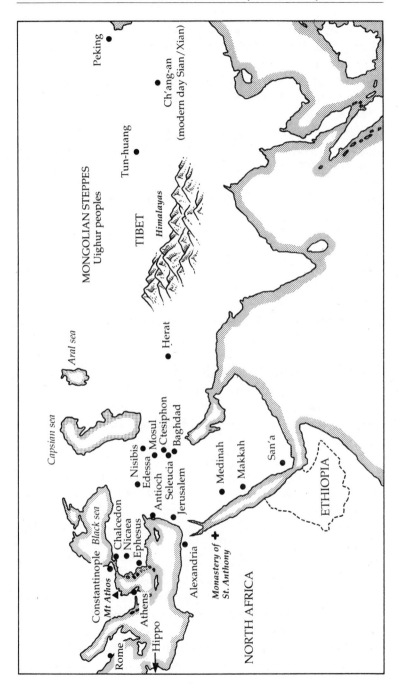

autonomy. The State promised certain support and protection in return for the support of the Church.

We have to journey back to Constantinople for the next stage in this strange story. For in 428, an outsider was elected Bishop of Constantinople (it did not become a Patriarchate until 451). His name was Nestorius and he came from Antioch, where he had gained a tremendous reputation as a preacher.

Nestorius saw himself as a defender of true Orthodoxy and as a result was against recent developments in the theology of the Church. He was also inclined through his training to look on human nature from a Pelagian viewpoint rather than in the way that Augustine of Hippo was preaching at the time. He was therefore positive in his evaluation of the human within the person of Christ and sought to elevate the human within the incarnation and so to balance it with the divine. The resulting theology is somewhat hard to determine, separated as we are by time and by the revisions of both his followers and those who opposed him. In essence, he seems to have taught that Jesus was a human being who was 'taken up' by the Spirit of God. This Spirit, known as the Word, bestowed a form of divinity upon Jesus, but that divinity did not affect the fact that he was in essence an ordinary human being like you or me. Thus Jesus was a man made God rather than God made man. However, this may be going too far. It is hard to tell.

Whatever the exact nature of Nestorius' beliefs about the way in which the divine and the human combined in Christ, we know one thing about his teaching. That was that he considered the relatively recent use of the title 'Mother of God' for the Virgin Mary to be heretical. The phrase had been in use in Egypt since the third century. Nestorius suspected this title for two reasons. First, it seemed to him to be overstating the divine and understating the human in Christ. Surely, he argued, the only title which could be used about Mary was 'Mother of Christ'. God could not have a mother, His second reason was that he feared that such a phrase smacked of goddess worship and that Mary would be revered as some form of female deity.

He was obviously concerned about the growth of the cult of Mary in Egypt. Here the old statues and forms ascribed to Isis, the great goddess of birth and rebirth who was usually shown cradling her son Horus, a god who was widely revered in Egypt, had transferred across to Mary, cradling Jesus. It was the goddess dimension of this imagery that made Nestorius speak out. There is an irony in this which reached its denouement on the edges of China four hundred years later (see below).

Nestorius was forced to defend this teaching when a chaplain of his preached that no one should use the term Mother of God. He went on to say that the term *Theotokos*, meaning 'God-bearer', was also heretical because all that one could say of Mary was that she bore Christ – *Christotokos*. Nestorius was immediately plunged into crisis. Cyril of Alexandria, a stout defender of the 'Mother of God' belief, and of the whole Alexandrian school which emphasized the divinity of Christ rather than his humanity, called upon the emperor to depose Nestorius. The argument became so heated that Emperor Theodosius II had to call a special council at Ephesus in 431 to resolve it. This council was a sordid affair, with neither side showing much in the way of Christian charity. The result, however, eventually went against Nestorius who was deposed and sent off into exile in Egypt where, some time between 440 and 450, he died in obscurity.

His teachings however did not die. In Edessa, that ancient centre of Eastern Christianity, the debate raged, with many in the great Academy of Edessa taking the side of Nestorius. This tension increased when, in reaction to the emphasis on the human in Nestorian thinking, there arose a powerful group claiming the opposite. Indeed, this group were so opposed to Nestorius' views that they ended up saying that there was nothing human in Christ – that he was in fact one person, and that divine. These Christians, called Monophysite because of their teaching of one nature, soon spread widely, even though they were opposed by the Orthodox of Constantinople. In Edessa, the debates grew extremely heated.

In 451 the emperor called a council at Chalcedon, which condemned the teachings of both Nestorius and the Monophysites. The effect of this was to divide the Eastern church straight down the middle. The Egyptian, Ethiopian, Syrian and the

Armenian churches declared for the Monophysite doctrine and hence forth were separated from the Byzantine Orthodox Church – a division which was only healed in the late 1980s.

In Edessa, the Monophysites took control of the great Academy and forced the Nestorian scholars out. These scholars fled east into the Persian Empire to escape persecution and found ready support for their teachings in the Eastern church and in the Persian Empire, which was only too happy at being able to spread discord amongst the Christians of the Roman Empire. The scholars established their academy at Nisibis, which was to be the intellectual centre of the Church for over 800 years.

The coming of Nestorian teachings to the Eastern church or the Church of Persia as it might well be called, meant that at last the Christians there could show that they were different from their Roman/Byzantine co-religionists. The threat of being considered as agents of Constantinople was thus overcome and the Church began to expand, and at a rate which is remarkable even today. Its success in establishing itself in Persia at a time when Byzantium and Christianity were seen by that country as the enemy was illustrated by an extraordinary sequence of events in the second and third decades of the seventh century.

BYZANTIUM AGAINST PERSIA

In the year 610, two men faced each other. In Constantinople, Heraclius had just been enthroned as emperor, while in Persia, Shah Chosroes II had drawn together a massive army to attack the Byzantine Empire. At first the Persians had it all their own way. From 611 onwards, province after province fell, and the greatest blow of all fell in 614. The Persians captured Palestine and for the first time since Constantine the Great 300 years before, the Christian holy places fell into the hands of non-believers.

The destruction of these holy of holies by the Zoroastrian army was unimaginably terrible. At the fall of Jerusalem, tens of thousands were put to death and the neighbourhood was so devastated that even today it has never recovered its former prosperity. Throughout Palestine, the great Christian shrines were totally destroyed, with one exception – the Church of the Nativity in Bethlehem. And why was this one church spared? For the simple reason that a mosaic over the main door showed the three wise men visiting Christ, and the wise men were dressed as Persian Zoroastrian sages.

In the sack of Jerusalem, the holy relics such as the true cross and the spear which wounded Jesus were seized – but not in order to be destroyed. Instead they were borne eastward with pomp and ceremony as a gift for the shah's queen. For the queen of this scourge of Byzantine Christianity was a Nestorian called Meryem. The relics were placed in her private chapel and venerated.

Once he had conquered Palestine and Syria, Chosroes proved to be a very even-handed ruler. He gave the Nestorians and Monophysites equal status with the Orthodox and ruled them fairly. In contrast, when Heraclius began his reconquest of the lands, the Orthodox church alone was favoured and the others were heavily taxed to finance the war. The war between Persia and Byzantium lasted until 628 when Heraclius triumphed over Chosroes, who was brutally murdered in a palace coup led by the son of his first wife, the Nestorian, Meryem. In 629 the relics of the true cross and the passion were handed back to a victorious Heraclius.

It is important to understand how un-imperial the Nestorian church was. It saw the imperial form of the faith – Byzantine Christianity – as its and its country's foe. While it had high status in Persia – witness Meryem – it was self-ruling and had grown to maturity under a system which favoured another faith, Zoroastrianism. It was thus a church of the minority which saw this as its role.

It was from this church that a remarkable emissary set out some time in 634 or 635 to travel to China to take the gospel to that land.

THE FAITH COMES TO CHINA

When T'ai Tsung, the accomplished Emperor [AD 627–649], was beginning his prosperous reign in glory and splendour, with intelligence and wisdom ruling the people, there was in the kingdom of Ta-ch'in a highly virtuous man called A-lo-pen. He augured from the blue sky and decided to carry the true Sutras with him, and watching the harmony of the winds, he hastened through difficulties and dangers. In the ninth year of Cheng-kuan [635] he came to Ch'ang-an. [The capital of the rising T'ang dynasty of China]. The Emperor despatched Duke Fang Hsuan-ling, his Minister of State, to take an escort to the western suburb to meet the guest and to bring him to the palace.

Thus does the Nestorian Stone of AD 781 tell the story of the arrival and reception of the missionary Alopen, bishop of the Nestorian church. The Nestorian Stone is a remarkable tablet standing some ten feet tall, inscribed in Chinese with some Syriac. It tells the story of the coming of Christianity to China in 635 and carries an account of its teachings. It is the most precious monument of the Nestorian church in China that we still have, and I shall discuss it in more detail on pp. 109–14.

The response of the emperor is interesting. He had the scriptures translated, and having read them issued a formal edict of toleration of the new religion, going so far as to erect a monastery for the bishop. So begins the strange story of Nestorian Christianity in China.

The formal greeting accorded Alopen is unusual. He was treated as if he were a mighty prince or the leader of a country and this has puzzled scholars. Why did the T'ang emperor consider this emissary of Christianity to be so important? Was it because he came from the West and China has always associated the spiritual world with the West (while the West has always looked East)? Or was it because he came from areas with which China wished to establish good relations? The T'ang dynasty was just beginning to consolidate its hold on a country which had been plagued by minor kingdoms and petty rulers for centuries, and was therefore beginning to look beyond its frontiers. Whatever the reason, Nestorian Christianity was welcomed into the court of the emperor and was given all assistance possible to spread. Its formal title was the Brilliant Teaching or Shining Teaching – a reference it is believed to the use of the imagery of light in Christianity.

From 635 to 845, the Nestorian Church spread far and wide, reaching, so one document says, every province of China. Certainly the Nestorian Stone gives evidence of a highly successful and well-adapted community, living in friendship and tolerance with the other cultures around them. Christian documents found in the Tunhuang caves in the early twentieth century, and dating from no later than the tenth century when the caves were sealed, also show a faith which has adapted itself to the language and insights of the culture in which it is functioning.

In 845, Taoist and Confucian scholars persuaded the emperor to issue an edict against all foreign religions. The foremost of these was Buddhism, which had over a quarter of a million monks and nuns; next came the Manichaeans, who were numerous because they had converted the Uighurs, who inhabited the area of Inner Mongolia and northern China, and whose vast and powerful empire lay to the north of the T'ang territories. Feared for nearly 200 years, the Uighur empire was collapsing by the 840s and the Chinese took revenge by closing all the Manichaean monasteries and persecuting the priests of the faith. At the same time, and in a general atmosphere of xenophobia, the Nestorian, Zoroastrian and Muslim centres of education were closed, with some 3000 Nestorian monks being returned to lay life.

With this persecution, the first wave of Nestorian Christianity died out. It seems to have struggled on in some places, but in the heartland of China it was virtually extinguished. Not so on the borders. In the area to the west of China, north of Tibet, there grew up an extraordinary culture where Buddhism, Shamanism and Christianity mixed. Here the Nestorians were very successful, with a number of the major tribes of Mongolians converting to Christianity some time in the tenth and eleventh centuries. The Nestorian presence in this area never ceased, for the persecution of 845 did not reach into these border lands. Here, on the edge of China, the strange mixture of groups led to a unique culture which drew almost equally upon Christianity, Buddhism and Manichaeism for its sustenance. This culture lasted from the ninth to the thirteenth centuries and from it came a surprising development.

THE VIRGIN MARY AND THE BUDDHA

Nestorius had protested at the Egyptian use of the term 'Mother of God' for the Virgin because he feared she would be venerated as a goddess. However, Nestorian Christians obviously venerated Mary as the mother of Christ and took statues of her with them. These statues and indeed much of the cult of Mary comes from the adoption of the cult of Isis and her son Horus from ancient Egyptian religion. The similarities between the statues and the language used to describe them both make this link almost certain.

On the pack horses and camels of the Nestorian missionaries and merchants, the Isis/Mary figure travelled east. In the borderland culture of the Christian-Buddhist-Manichaean states of the Mongolians, the image was encountered by a faith, Buddhism, which had very little within it of the feminine. The Buddha had not even wanted women to be in his monastic orders, but he was eventually persuaded. But Buddhism is an archetypal male religion in which only the Buddha's mother features in any way as being a woman of religious significance. This made for a rather unhelpful faith, especially as far as the Mongolians and Chinese were concerned. With their deep shamanistic roots, men and women played key roles in all aspects of their popular religion.

However, contained within Indian Buddhism was the idea of a semi-deity of compassion who offered help and assistance to struggling humanity. In the Sanskrit texts, he is called Avalokitesvara, which was translated into Chinese as Kuan-yin, which means the one who hears. This deity was masculine right up until the tenth century, though from the late eighth century onwards, the idea of a female deity also called Kuan-yin spread from Tibet. By the eleventh century, the statues of Kuan-yin showed a woman who frequently carried a baby in her arms. This female, child-bearing, compassionate goddess has become the most popular deity, not just in Chinese Buddhism, but in Chinese folk religion. The statues first begin to appear in those areas where the Nestorians were existing in close association with the Buddhists, namely northern Tibet, southern Mongolia and western China. It would appear that it is in part due to the spread of Nestorian Christianity that the male deity of Kuan-yin became female and came to resemble the Virgin Mary and the Christ child.

ISLAM AND THE MONGOLS

In 634, the new religion of Islam began its dramatic movement out from its homeland of Arabia. In 637 and 638, the Muslims defeated the Persian armies, or what was left of them after Heraclius' victories, and Islam took control of the whole area.

This was not a great disaster at first for Nestorian Christianity, for once again, they were able to show that they had nothing to do politically with either the conquered Persian dynasty and its state religion Zoroastrianism, or the Byzantine Empire and its Orthodox church. Furthermore, Christianity, along with Judaism, was mentioned in the Qur'an with favour. So, obviously with some upheavals, the Nestorians settled down to live exactly as they had done under the shahs, namely as a self-governing community whose leaders were held accountable to the Muslim rulers for the loyalty of their people.

However, the upheavals did make it more difficult for them to communicate with their own faithful in China and Mongolia. The Muslim armies pushed further and further east towards China, creating havoc on the old Silk Roads, the vitally important routes across the deserts and mountains of central Asia, down which trade from and to China passed.

Only gradually, however, did Islam become a religious as opposed to a political opponent in these areas. For many centuries, the Muslims were prepared to rule over subject peoples in the Persian/Monogolian and Chinese zones, not trying to convert them, but equally not stopping them if they wished to join Islam. During this time, Manichaeism, Buddhism and Christianity seem to have flourished on the edges of China.

As I have said, Nestorian Christianity had never been an imperial or state religion. It thus was able to spread far and wide because it carried virtually no cultural baggage with it, as we shall see in the Chinese materials it produced. However, as the faith began to win over entire tribes such as the Keraits, the Merkites and large sections of the Uighurs, it began to have a sort of state church role. This was very much mixed up with elements of the pre-Christian faith of shamanism, in a way not dissimilar to the incorporation of druidic dimensions into Celtic Christianity.

The significance of Christianity in the Mongolian tribes is seen in the fact that Genghis Khan's mother was a Nestorian, as were many of his generals and administrators. Indeed, it was with the conquering Mongolian hordes that Nestorian Christianity returned to China proper, but this time as one of the faiths of a conquering power. The Nestorian church soon reconstituted itself right across northern China and when Marco Polo made his epic journey in the late thirteenth century, he met Nestorians at virtually every city he visited, and the patriarch of the Nestorian church in Baghdad appointed an archbishop for Peking.

Islam had gradually been gaining ground over the centuries, converting various of the tribes. With the invasion of Persia by the Mongol tribes, there came a turning point, as the Mongolian hordes hesitated between converting to Christianity or to Islam. The tribes had gradually coalesced around the dynamic figure of Genghis Khan, and it had been under his brilliant military leadership that they had swept down upon China at the beginning of the thirteenth century. As I have said, his mother was a Nestorian and the great leader of the western Mongolian horde, Batu, was very favourably disposed to Nestorian Christianity. Emissaries were requested from the pope to come and convert the Mongols and an alliance between the Mongols and

Christendom was proposed to crush the Muslim forces between. But the Nestorian church was not able to make the necessary transition from being one faith amongst many to becoming the state religion of such a vast empire. The initiative was lost and the Mongolian horde slowly became a Muslim force.

But the Mongolians were still favourable towards Nestorian Christianity. They allowed it many privileges, as the remarkable journey of two Mongolian priests to the Holy Land in the 1270s bears witness. This journey marks the apogee of the story. They set out from the cathedral at Peking (Khan-Balik as it was called) with the express blessing of Kublai Khan. Both were monks, one called Sawma and the other Markos. Both were senior in the Church in Peking and both wished to make a pilgrimage to Jerusalem.

After many adventures, they arrived in Baghdad. Here Markos was elected Patriarch of the Nestorian church and ruled as Patriarch Yahbh-Allaha III from 1281 to 1317. During his reign the Nestorian church was at its most powerful and widespread ever. Meanwhile Sawma was sent as an ambassador to the West. He visited Constantinople and Rome and eventually reached as far west as France and the court of the English king, Edward I where at the express wish of the king, this Nestorian monk from Peking celebrated Holy Communion for the whole court.

This remarkable story deserves a book of its own, and we are fortunate in still having a text of the account of the monks journey written during their lifetime. Suffice it to say that I can think of no better illustration of the remarkable spread and respect which the Nestorian church had achieved at this time than this story of the Nestorian monk Sawma from Peking being sent by Kublai Khan and being received by King Edward I of England.

But the Nestorian church was at this point at its peak, a peak from which it descended very swiftly. Unable to hold their own against the Muslims, the Nestorians gradually lost control of the Mongolian tribes who converted either to Buddhism or to Islam. In China they were a foreign faith now, brought in by the hated Mongols and as such they were swept aside when the Chinese rose against the Mongols and established a fiercely Chinese dynasty, the Ming, in 1368.

The final blow to this once vast non-imperial church, was the invasion of Timur the Lame, known as Tamerlane in Western sources. From the 1370s until the start of the fifteenth century. Tamerlane and his tribal armies of Turks and Mongols carved out an empire from northern China to Moscow and from Delhi to the edges of Palestine. In doing so, he massacred millions and totally destroyed the old Persian culture, including much of the culture of Islam and of course, the Nestorians. The few Nestorian Christians who survived his attacks fled to the mountains of Kurdistan, which is where they are to be found today.

So ended what began as an attempt to impose orthodoxy on the Orthodox church of Constantinople, was then exiled and finally taken up by the Eastern church covering a larger area in its missionary activity than any other branch of the Christian faith up to the European migrations and conquests of the sixteenth century.

Why is it of interest today? Because it travelled these vast distances unencumbered by religious, linguistic or philosophical baggage from Greece or from Rome; because it was never a vehicle of imperialism or the State until just towards its end in China; and because it was able to develop an expression of Christianity which spoke within the cultures which it encountered, and which was able to live with and indeed absorb much from those cultures and from the other faiths around it. It was the most successful example to date of Christianity in dialogue and creative interaction with other faiths and cultures. It never conquered. With the exception of some Mongolian tribes, it never dominated, but was always a presence within the wider community. It was also capable of giving to other religions.

THE CHINESE GOSPEL

Let us now look at how Nestorian Christianity adapted itself to Chinese society and culture. As there are no extant Christian buildings of the Nestorian period left in China, and only a few of the beautiful Nestorian crosses, it is to the writings that we turn, in much the same way as it is possible to enter the world of the Celtic Christians through their prayers.

The most succinct description of Christianity that has come down from the Chinese Nestorians is to be found beautifully carved on the Nestorian Stone. We can be sure that the terminology used here was that accepted as authoritative by the Church in China, because the monk who wrote this treatise on Christianity was called Ching-ching, also known as the monk Adam. He will feature to a very large extent in the composition of the later texts, and he was also a crucial link between Christianity and Buddhism.

The Nestorian Stone

The Nestorian Stone opens with a discourse on the essential teachings of Christianity. From this it moves on to describe the Church and some of its rituals, especially those which were unfamiliar to the Chinese world, such as striking a wooden plank to call the faithful to worship. This method is still used in Orthodox monasteries in Greece, and has also passed into use in many Chinese Buddhist monasteries.

After a description of the monks and priests (who it is noted, do not keep slaves, male or female because they treat all people, both the powerful and the lowly, as equal), it moves on to tell of the arrival of Alopen in 635 and his reception. Then follows a translation of the imperial edict of recognition issued in 638 in which the arrival of Christianity from the west is linked with the story of Lao Tzu, founder of the Taoists, who rode west to seek wisdom. Now, says the stone, this wisdom has come east to us.

There then follows a brief topographical and economic outline of where Ta-ch'in — the phrase used to cover the Roman

Empire and parts of Persia — lies and what it makes. This is
followed by a brief history of the main events in the life of the
Church in China. We are told that the next emperor after Tai
Tsung, Kao Tsung, favoured the Christians and built monasteries in all provinces, and the faith spread to every city. Later, in
or around 697, Christians were persecuted and the monastic and
spiritual life of the Church was disrupted. However, the efforts
of Lo-Han, head of the monks, and Chi-lieh, both Christians
from the west, restored the Church.

Under the Emperor Hsuan Tsung (713–756) the church was
greatly favoured and honoured. Priests were even invited to
perform services before the emperor himself and many churches
and monasteries were endowed and beautified. After him came
Su Tsung (756–763), who built four new monasteries and
refounded monasteries in the north-western city of Ling-wu
(modern day Ling Chou in Kansu). Finally, it pays respect to the
ruling emperor, T'ai Tsung, who seems to have been well
disposed towards the Church.

There then follows praise for the sponsors of the Church and
for those who gave generously to it. In particular the priest
I-ssu, a powerful member of the imperial court, is highlighted.
In terminology which almost exactly echoes the description of
the sheep in the parable of the sheep and the goats in Matthew
25, he is described thus:

> He bade the hungry come and fed them; he bade the cold come and
> clothed them; he healed the sick and raised them up; he buried the
> dead and laid them to rest.

This is then followed by a distillation in verse of the previous
sections of the stone, which ends with a terse outline of the
reason for mission. Finally the monument ends with a long list
of priests, bishops, monks and archdeacons involved with the
stone.

The most interesting parts of the text are those which outline
Christian teaching. The rest is fascinating historically, but it is
the understanding of the Christian gospel in China that is of

greatest importance to us. The text opens with an outline of the faith. Christianity was called the 'Brilliant Teaching of Ta-ch'in':

A monument commemorating the diffusion throughout the Middle Kingdom [China] of the Brilliant Teaching of Ta-ch'in.

Recorded by Ching-ching, a monk of the Ta-ch'in monastery [then in Syriac, the language of the Nestorian church] - Adam, priest and country-bishop and papa of Zinistan.

Behold! The One who is unchanging, who being Uncreated is the Origin of the origins; the inaccessible in spiritual purity, existing beyond the last of the last; who holds the mysterious origin of life and creates all things, who in his glory imparts his mysterious nature to all sages; is this not the mysterious Persons of our Three in One, the uncreated Lord of the Universe, A-lo-he? [Alohe appears to be the closest the Chinese could get to the Syriac word for God, Allaha – from which the Islamic/Arabic word Allah also comes].

He set out the figure of ten [in Chinese ten is written with a cross] to define the four quarters; he set the original breath in motion and produced the two principles of Nature [yin and yang]. The dark void was transformed and Heaven and Earth appeared. He made and perfected all things; he created the first man. He gave him special goodness and an even temperament, he gave to him dominion over the ocean of creatures. This original nature was humble, empty of all selfishness, free from all complexity of lust and passion. It came to pass that So-tan propagated falsehood, borrowing the adornment of the pure spirit. He insinuated [the idea of] equal greatness [with God] into the original good; he introduced [the theory of] the mysterious identity [of being and not-being] into the evil that had resulted.

As a result of this, 365 sects arose in quick succession and left deep furrows behind. They struggled to weave nets of the laws with which to trap the innocent. Some pointed to natural objects claiming that they were the right things to worship; others denied the reality of existence and insisted on ignoring the duality; some sought to call down blessings by means of prayers and sacrifices, yet others boasted of their own goodness and treated others with contempt. The minds of the people became confused; they were never at rest, but to no avail. The heat of their distress became a scorching flame and thus blinded by self, they only deepened the darkness, lost their way and were unable to return home.

Because of this the divided person of our Three in One, the brilliant and revered Mi-shih-he [Messiah], veiling his true majesty, came to earth as man. An angel proclaimed the good news. A virgin gave birth to the sage in Ta-ch'in. A bright star announced the good news. Persians saw its glory and came to offer gifts. He fulfilled the ancient law of the twenty-four sages [Old Testament writers], governing the State on the great principle. He founded the new teaching of non-assertion which operates silently through the Holy Spirit of the Three in One and made humanity capable of good works by following the truth. Establishing the standard of the Eight conditions, he purified human nature and perfected truth. He opened wide the Three constant gates [the senses], celebrating life and destroying death. He hung up a brilliant sun to take by storm the halls of darkness. The forces of evil were all defeated. He rowed the boat of mercy and travelled to the palaces of light. In this way were all sentient beings saved. His mighty work completed, he ascended at midday to his original place.

The text then describes certain practices of the Christians and concludes this section with the following:

The true and eternal way is wonderful and yet hard to name. Its benefits and purpose are clearly known and splendid, therefore we name it and call it the Brilliant Teaching. Yet the way without a prophet will not flourish; a prophet without the way will not be great. When way and prophet match and tally, all creation is civilized and enlightened.

The only other section which is of interest in this context is the final part of the poetic rendition of the text. It reads:

> How vast and extensive is the Truth [or Way],
> Yet how minute and mysterious it is,
> Making an effort to name it,
> We call it the Three in One
> The Lord is able to do anything,
> The servants are ready to preach,
> Therefore we set up this noble monument
> And praise the great blessings.

The text of the Nestorian Stone is redolent with Taoist

imagery, texts from Chinese classics such as the *Tao Te Ching* and *I Ching*, and elements of Chinese Buddhism. It also carries with it certain Greek notions. Its opening would not have raised an eyebrow amongst the Orthodox bishops at one of the councils which agreed the creeds. It is the platonic God, before all and removed from all. As such, it fitted with some of the philosophical schools of China which had tried to determine whether there was a supreme being.

Then we come to the first Chinese element: the notion that God was the origin of the origin. This very much picked up on Taoist philosophical thought, which saw the Tao as being the origin of the origin – an idea which is developed in the second half of the *Tao Te Ching*. Quite soon after that we come to the idea of yin and yang, the two elemental forces which Chinese cosmology had posited as being the fundamental elements of the universe. Total opposites of each other – black and white, male and female etc. – they were seen not as divine forces but as the essential nature of reality.

We then return to standard Christian theology about humanity being given dominion – remember, Nestorian Christianity was an urban faith and thus very much lived in the world where humanity fashioned and shaped what it wanted from the raw elements of nature, unlike the Celts who lived in a much closer relationship with nature. However, true to the more Pelagian understanding of human nature, there is no sense that Adam's sin has irredeemably tainted all humanity, no doctrine of original sin, but much more a sense of people who have lost sight of that which they once saw clearly. The outline of the different ways people respond to the crisis of alienation from God or the search for an answer to life is very vividly presented and no doubt was meant to refer to faiths and cults practised at the time.

It is when we come to the person and purpose of Christ that there is a real shift. Here is a presentation of his coming which is Celtic both in its vision of Christ working as part of the harmony of the 'Three in One', and in its view of Christ being a compassionate 'One' who rescues souls and guides them to eternity. There is no actual mention of the crucifixion, unless the passage 'He hung up a brilliant sun to take by storm the halls of darkness' is an allusion to it, which it may well be. In other words, the Chinese Nestorians saw Christ's death as part of the overall purpose of compassionate rescue, not as a defeat turned to glory or a sign of human sinfulness. The language used here to describe the rescue of souls is entirely Buddhist in origin, just as in Augustine or Anselm, terminology from Roman law was used to define the meaning of Christ. I would argue that neither of them is 'right' or 'wrong'. The question must always be, does the language or imagery thus employed, regardless of its origin, do justice to the meaning of Christ?

The lack of 'guilt' about the crucifixion and the absence of any original sin, led as far as one can tell, to a much more cheerful form of Christianity than that to be found in the Roman church. What is obvious from other texts is that Jesus was seen and experienced as a divine teacher who illuminated the Way, or who rowed souls to safety, rather than as someone upon whom sins were laid and who suffered as a result. Indeed there is little that I have seen in Chinese Nestorian texts which deals with suffering as such. What is taught is that life is precarious and that Christ, in charity, gave up his life to save all people.

The final two sections, which are very similar, are based on texts in the *Tao Te Ching* in which the difficulty of naming the way is spoken of (see chapter 1 of the *Tao Te Ching*), and the notion that you can have a sage but not have the wisdom and vice versa introduced. The language used makes it very clear that a well-read person would immediately see the links to classic, Taoist philosophy.

The Christianity of the Nestorian Stone had taken upon itself a very Chinese hue. At first some of it seems very strange. But it is important to remember that any of the original disciples of Jesus or earliest members of the Church would have felt that Augustine's theology or the language of the Nicene Creed was equally strange. Just as Greek thought clothed the mystery of the incarnation in terms comprehensible to itself, so did Chinese Christianity.

The Nestorian Sutras

I want to look at three more texts from China. The first comes from somewhere around 800; the second from the very start of the Nestorian mission – so mid-seventh century; and the third comes from the end of the eighth century and is believed to be from the same pen as the Nestorian Stone, namely that of Ching-ching, Adam the priest. The first one is a hymn in adoration of the 'Three in One', and is based on the Syrian version of what we know in the West as the *Gloria in Excelsis*. Being based on an extant text, it holds more nearly to what we know as standard Christian terminology, yet it manages to draw in Chinese ideas and to turn the hymn into the sort of philosophical discourse and poem so beloved by both Taoist and Buddhist philosophers.

A HYMN OF THE BRILLIANT TEACHING TO THE THREE MAJESTIES FOR OBTAINING SALVATION

The highest heavens with deepest reverence adore you.
The great earth dwells upon your peace and harmony.
Humanity's true nature is founded in you,
A-lo-ha the merciful Father of the Three Powers.

All good people worship you in sincerity.
All the enlightened ones sing praises.
All who have souls trust and depend upon you
Receiving holy and merciful light to free them from evil.

Hard to find, impossible to reach, upright, true, eternal.
Merciful Father, Shining Son, Pure Wind King,
Amongst all rulers, you are the Master Ruler;
Amongst all the world honoured ones, you are the Emperor of
    Law.

The eternal existence mysteriously lightens the infinite,
The brilliant majesty thoroughly probes the boundaries of the
    finite,
Since the beginning of time, no-one has seen you,
Nor can any imagine you.

Alone completely perfect in clear holy virtue,

Alone divinely majestic in unmeasured strength,
Alone unchanging and existing in majesty,
The root and origin of all goodness, without end.

We now call to mind your Mercy and Grace,
Sighing for your mysterious joy to enlighten our realm,
Honoured Mi-shih-he most holy Son,
Widely delivering, saving countless souls from suffering.

Merciful joyful Lamb of the everlasting King of Life,
Generally and universally having compassion for all who suffer,
     you do not hesitate to help,
Take away the weight of sins of all the living.
And restore their souls that they may be secure.

The Holy Son sits in honour on the throne on the Father's right
     hand,
His throne is exalted higher than others.
Great Master be willing to answer our prayers,
Send down the raft to grant escape from the tossing on the stream
     of fire.

The great Master is our merciful Father,
The great Master is our holy Lord,
The great Master is our spiritual king,
The great Master is universal saviour and deliverer.

The great Master with wisdom helps all the weary,
All eyes look up without ceasing,
And you send down sweet dew upon the withered and parched,
So that all living things may be watered and the root of goodness
     be refreshed.

Most holy universally honoured Mi-shih-he,
We adore the merciful Father: the ocean-treasure of mercy,
Most holy; and the humble, and holy spirit nature.
Clear and powerful is the law, beyond all philosophy.

The hymn while being very clearly rooted in classical Christian
thought, is also a mixture of images taken from Manichaeism,
Buddhism and Taoism. As such, it is obviously trying to use
such terms in order to make the overt Christian ideas intelligible
to the sophisticated Chinese reader.

     The text opens in a way immediately recognizable to any

Christian reader familiar with either the *Gloria in Excelsis* or with some of the psalms such as Pss. 148 or 150. The last line of the first verse mingles Christian and Buddhist/Taoist imagery. Here God is referred to as A-lo-ha, which is the term for an arhat or lo-han in Buddhism. This term is close to the Syriac word for God, Allaha, but also seems to be a deliberate attempt to find a religiously significant word close to the Syriac. It is in fact not a wholly appropriate one but Christianity has had great difficulty finding an appropriate term in Chinese to express the notion of a supreme yet personal God.

The arhat is one of the enlightened ones who fully comprehends the truth and nature of the universe. Here the term is used with a classic Christian term of the Father, who is then pictured as being the Father of the 'Three Powers.' In classical Chinese philosophy and religion, this means the triad of Heaven, Earth and Humanity. In this formula Chinese philosophy summed up all existence and put humanity in a pivotal position of maintaining the balance between Heaven and Earth — between the yin and the yang. Yin and yang are opposite forces whose ability to co-exist is found in their perpetual struggle to dominate the other — a dominance which can never be achieved but whose dynamism keeps the world spinning. Humanity's role is to ensure that the balance of powers between these two opposites is kept in true equation. In thus combining Buddhist arhats with Christian ideas of the creator Father and classical Chinese cosmology, the translator has managed to bring together the range of faiths and cultures within which he is operating, in an unusual and fairly successful way.

In the terminology of the trinity, the translator uses terms identical to those used by the Manichaeans in their translations into Chinese. It is also identical to the terminology of the Nestorian Stone. (There is an interesting issue — not appropriate to this book — of what happened to Manichaean beliefs as they entered China and what level of interaction there was between Christianity and Manichaeanism — both alien faiths; both struggling to find appropriate terms. The overall effect seems to have been to bring Manichaean beliefs more into line with key Christian beliefs. But this is a subject for another book!) The passage 'Send down the raft to grant escape' is a direct borrowing from the Buddhist imagery of the Buddha offering a vehicle for escape from the trials of rebirth. Here it is placed into a more Christian concept of escape from the sufferings of this earthly life.

The hymn, whilst using Buddhist and Taoist terminology, is very clearly still working within confines set by classical Christianity, albeit that it is taking these and reworking them in a new cultural context. The next document does something more radical. It takes the story of Christ and puts it within the literary and religious norms of Chinese society and culture of the seventh century. The actual translation was done very early on in the history of Christianity in China, perhaps as one of the initial documents which the emperor ordered translated in 635. The Chinese is at times very cumbersome and even unintelligible, but this does not distract from the uniqueness of what was attempted. For in this document, the *Hsu-t'ing Mi-shih-he Sutra*– 'The Jesus-Messiah Sutra', the life of Christ and its significance, are presented in a thoroughly Chinese literary way, using many terms taken straight from Taoism and Buddhism. It is a fascinating glimpse at how the gospel sounds in a totally un-Graeco-Roman culture. As it is quite long (206 verses) I am unable to reproduce all of it here. I have therefore tried to select those parts which make most interesting reading.

The text opens in a classical Chinese Buddhist way, with the Messiah pictured serenely teaching, exactly as the Buddha is shown in Buddhist texts, which emphasizes his divine teaching role rather than his earthly life.

At that time, preaching the laws of Yahweh, the Lord of Heaven, the Messiah said:

There may be different views, but who can teach about the admirable wonder of the meaning of the sutras?

Who can tell where the Lord of Heaven dwelt before his revelation? What really was the place where he lived until then?

All the Buddhas as well as guardian deities and spirits and Arhats can see the Lord of Heaven.

No human being however has ever seen the Lord of Heaven living amongst the people.

Who has there ever been, godly enough to see the Lord of Heaven?

This is because the Lord of Heaven is like the wind in appearance, and who has seen the wind?

The Lord of Heaven is incessantly crossing the world and is present everywhere at all time.

Because of this, everyone existing in the world, lives and exists through the strength of the Lord of Heaven.

This passage uses terms which are a mixture of transliteration such as Yahweh; straight adoption of Christian imagery, like the idea of the Spirit being like a wind which blows where it wishes; and Taoist philosophical language about the Tao or Way which are then adapted to speak of God, for example the last line which echoes many similar lines within the *Tao Te Ching* such as chapter 34. The text then continues by talking further about the parallels between the Lord of Heaven and the wind, and how impossible it is to see the Lord of Heaven. After a brief piece on how the good are rewarded and the wicked punished, we come to the following:

All sins have come into the world because our original ancestor committed the sin of disobedience in the Garden of seed and fruit bearing trees.

Therefore, all living beings should consider the consequences of actions in previous times.

But the Lord of Heaven himself received the bitter suffering and then, for the first time, he was able to keep all living things from falling.

This interpretation of the passion of Christ is very much in keeping with what we have seen earlier. The purpose of Christ's passion is seen as being that he entered into the experience of suffering pain which afflicts all people. Thus and only thus was Christ able to comprehend suffering fully and thereby to show that life continues through even such suffering. There then follows a rather contorted section which takes the first two commandments and applies them to the usefulness of respecting, or even venerating, the emperor – a clear nod in the direction of classic Confucian values. We then come to an exposition of the consequences of Christian life – the discipline that should be expected of Christians. It reflects very closely the texts of books such as the *Didarch*, one of the earliest books of Christian life and discipline

This section opens in a slighty confused way with the Ten Commandments, set out in a way very similar to the Five Precepts or Commandments of Buddhism. What is interesting is that some of the basic commandments have been given a broader or more universal meaning; the fourth and fifth, for example show that we should have compassion on all life, not just human life. This is echoed in some of the very late, apocryphal gospels such as the Gospel of Peace of Jesus Christ which is known to us in two texts, one in Aramaic and the other in old Slavonic, which Nestorian monks fleeing from the Mongols brought west in the thirteenth century. The text says:

The first thing is to obey the Lord of Heaven . . .

The second vow is to act in filial piety and to care for parental needs with true sincerity. All the people who follow the Heaven-Way will make their home there when they die, if they are filial to their father and mother and do not fail to obey what they are told.

So we should serve our father and mother for no living thing exists without a mother and father.

[The third commandment is lost.]

The fourth vow is that anyone who professes faith in the precepts should thus be kind and good to all living beings and should neither hate anyone, nor harbour evil thoughts about them.

The fifth vow is that all people should not only not take life, but should persuade others to do likewise, for the life of all living beings is of equal value to the lives of humans.

The sixth vow is that none should commit adultery with another's wife, nor use any persuasion to try and make her commit adultery.

The seventh vow is that no one should steal.

The eighth vow is that no one should covet another's riches or rank when they see them, nor should they covet his field, house or servants.

The ninth vow is that none should plot to bear false witness against another who is happier than he.

The tenth vow is that no one should serve the Lord of Heaven with anything which does not belong to that person or at another person's expense.

Beside these there are many other things which you should consider.

You should not deceive another person by taking advantage of his defencelessness; if you happen to see a poor child, you should not turn away from him; if your enemy is hungry, you should feed him and give him drink in plenty as well as forgive him and then forget what it was that caused you to make him your enemy.

If you happen to see someone having to work very hard, you should assist him and use your own power for his good, as well as give him a drink of milk; if you happen to see another person without clothing, you should give him clothes.

Those who have received the precepts should be humble and never hate another.

Let all the people awaken to good deeds and stop thinking about evil, for if we do good, we shall have less condemnation. Let therefore, everyone do good deeds constantly for the sake of humanity.

All the living beings have turned their face away from the Lord and committed sins and finally rebelled against the Lord of Heaven.

Seeing that this was how they all lived, the Lord of Heaven had compassion for them and told them to do good and not to remain caught in the corrupt ways.

The Lord of Heaven therefore caused the Cool Wind [Holy Spirit] to enter a virgin named Mo-yen [Mary].

There then follows the familiar story of the birth and early life of Jesus, with a few odd additions such as: 'There were however some ignorant people who said that if the Cool Spirit had made the virgin pregnant and caused her to have a son, then such a child must be the bottom of the world.' The story unfolds, from the visit to the temple when Jesus was twelve, through the baptism including even a statement in which the so-called 'hidden years' of Jesus, from twelve to thirty, are covered: 'The Messiah from the twelfth year of his age until he was a little over thirty-two years old sought out all who were evil and made them return to the good life and the right way.'

The passion of Christ is told in great detail from the time of his arrest. We hear nothing about Palm Sunday nor about the Last Supper. Instead we have a most movingly told version of the last hours of Jesus:

When he was over thirty-two years old, those who were the most wicked came into the presence of the Great King P'i-lo-tu-ssu and were able to say before P'i-lo-tu-ssu himself:

'The Messiah should be done to death. O Great King, do away with him at once!'

These followers of the wicked cause of existence all bore witness against the Messiah saying before the Great King P'i-lo-tu-ssu:

'The Messiah should be punished, indeed he should be put to death.'

Hearing this, the Great King wished to act justly in the case of such a man and said:

I have heard nothing of any crime which justifies the punishment of death nor have I seen anything to justify such action. This man does not deserve to die. Let this issue be resolved by those followers of the wicked cause of existence.'

The Great King went on:

'I cannot kill this man.'

Then those followers of the wicked cause of existence said:

'If this man is not punished with death, what will happen to us, both men and women?'

The Great King P'i-lo-tu-ssu ordered water to be brought to him and he washed his hands before them and came and stood before them and said:

'I can discover no reason to kill this man.'

Then those followers of the wicked cause of existence implored the King over and over again to do as they requested. They beseeched him so long and so intensely that he found he could not save this man.

The Messiah gave up his body to these wicked ones to be sacrificed for the sake of humanity: thus did he make the whole world to know that a human life is as precarious as a candle flame.

Thus in charity did he give up his life for the sake of all humanity, suffering death for them.

The Messiah at last gave his own body willingly to death.

These wicked people caught the Messiah and brought him to the place set apart and, after they had washed his hair, they led him to the placard place named Chi-chu [Golgotha].

Here they bound him upon the tree between two highwaymen, one being on his right, the other on his left.

That day on which they bound the Messiah upon the tree at the fifth hour, was the sixth day feast.

It was at dawn that they bound the Messiah upon the tree, but by the time the sun came towards west, there was deepest darkness on every side, and the very earth quaked and the mountains were torn apart and all the gates of the grave throughout the world were burst open and life returned to us all.

Seeing these things, how can anyone doubt what is written in the sutras?

Sadly, the text breaks off a few words further on. But it is an extraordinary text — extraordinary because of the language and words it uses. Here is Jesus, readily recognizable from the Gospels. Here are sections of his teachings and the teachings of the Old Testament — the Ten Commandments — and the account from Matthew 25 of caring for the hungry and the naked. But here also is a Christ who speaks for all living creatures; who calls for all life to be respected because the rest of existence is as precious as we are. Here are incidents in the story of Jesus not recorded in the gospels, such as the hair-washing at Golgotha.

Remember that this was not a text written in Chinese. This was a Chinese translation of one of the precious books brought almost certainly by Bishop Alopen. Here was the core teaching and life story of the Messiah as the Nestorian church wished to impart it to the Chinese. It is a remarkable piece of work, for all the inadequacies of the Chinese text at times.

Bishop Ching-ching and the Chinese Gospel

We now need to turn finally to the most enigmatic character in the story of the Nestorian church in China, Bishop Ching-ching, also known as Adam.

We know quite a lot about this priest. We know he wrote the text of the Nestorian monument, which means that as far as the church hierarchy was concerned in 781, he was the most appropriate man to express the views and teachings of the faith. We also find him named as the translator of thirty books, listed in a profile of the sacred books of the Church, a document called the *Book of Praise* which also lists the saints to whom prayers should be offered. At the end of this list, compiled it is thought in the tenth century, when the church was still functioning in the area of northern Tibet, Mongolia and eastern China, is the following:

> Hereby, with great respect, we declare that we examined the list of all the sutras and have found that there are in all 530 sutras belonging to this Religion of Ta-ch'in. They are, however, all on leave sheets in the Brahmin language. In the ninth year of the Chen-kuan period in the reign of the Emperor T'ai-tsung of the T'ang, Priest Alopen, Bishop of the Western Lands, arrived in the Middle Kingdom [China] and humbly presented a petition to the Throne in his native tongue.
>
> Fang Hsuan-ling and Wei Cheng reverentially submitted the matter to the Imperial Information, when the petition was translated.
>
> Afterwards, by Imperial Orders, the priest Ching-ching, Bishop of this Religion was summoned and the above thirty mentioned books were translated.

We also have a very odd piece of information from a Buddhist book. The book *Catalogue of the Teachings of Sakya During the Chen-yuan Period*, tells that a Buddhist scholar called Prajna came from Afghanistan to China via the sea and the port of Canton. It then reads as follows:

> He translated, together with Ching Ching Adama Persian priest, of the monastery, of Ta-ch'in, the Satparamitra Sutra from a Hu text [Uighur] and finished translating seven volumes. But because at this

time Prajna was not familiar with the Hu language nor understood Chinese, and because Ching Ching did not know Sanskrit nor was versed in the teachings of Sakya, so, though they pretended to be translating the text, yet they did not in reality obtain a half of its gems. They were seeking vainglory, privately and wrongly trying their luck. They presented a memorial, hoping to get it propagated. The emperor T'ai-tsung, who was intelligent, wise and accomplished, who revered the canon of Sakya, examined what they had translated and found the principles contained in it were obscure and the wording was diffused. Moreover the Sangharama of the Sakya and the monastery of Ta-ch'in differing very much in their customs and their practices being entirely opposed to one another, Ching Ching Adam handing down the teachings of Mi-shi-ho while the Shakyaputriya Sramans propagated the Sutras of the Buddha. It is to be wished that the boundaries of the doctrines be kept distinct and their followers may not intermingle. Orthodoxy and heterodoxy are different things, just as the rivers King and Wei have a different course.

These events took place in 787. It is important to note that while Ching-ching was obviously very interested in the texts of Buddhism, he was clearly seen as a Christian and the teachings of Christianity and Buddhism were noted as being very distinct from each other. The reason it is important to remember this is because the final text is one from the pen of Ching-ching himself. It is a translation again, of an original book called in Chinese the *Chih-hsuan-an-lo Sutra*, meaning 'the Sutra which aims at Mysterious Rest and Joy'. In other words, Ching-ching is not just making up a text. What he is certainly doing, however, is trying to express the Christian faith in a way which relates to his Chinese audience. Again, this is a long though complete text, containing 105 verses, many of which are quite extensive. It is probably the most 'Buddhist' rendition of the teachings of Christ ever written. I hope the extracts give some idea of its nature.

In true Buddhist style, it features a question and answer session between Jesus and Simon Peter. In Buddhist texts these sessions often take place between the Buddha and his favourite disciple Ananda. Here the model is followed almost exactly.

At the head of the crowd, Simon Peter rose up and placing his forearms across his heart, adored the Messiah and said, 'We the people have lived in error for so long. Unless there is some way in which we can be saved and protected, how can any sentient being achieve the Way of Rest and Joy?'

The Messiah answered him and said, 'Excellent is your question, excellent is your question. If there is any living creature who wants to be a partaker in the blessing of the Victorious Law, you must listen carefully to what I shall say.'

There then follows a rather technical discussion of the notions of motion and desire as obstacles to spiritual progress. This part contains a rather fine analogy. Jesus is talking about how the truth and the true way can be hidden and lost:

For instance, it may be compared to the reflection of the moon in a pond. If the water is muddy, then the image of the moon cannot be seen for that reason. It can be compared to a fire in a heap of grass. If the grass is wet, the fire will not be able to burn brightly for that one reason. So it is with the essence of life, which can become as sunk and hidden as these.

The text proceeds to recommend stillness and cutting off from all that thus muddies the water or dampens the grass.

If you could cut yourselves off from things that defile you, then you could be pure as the State of Pure-Emptiness itself. Then you would send forth the life-giving light that enlightens all livings things. Because this light enlightens all things, it is called the Way of Rest and Joy.

And again, let it be known Simon Peter that I am in all Heavens. I am in all the earth. Sometimes I am in the way leading to the grave, sometimes I am among the living.

I have to protect and carry all those who are of God [literally belong to the virtuous or righteous cause of existence].

In this section, we have almost straight Buddhist imagery such as in the last line, combined with Johannine theology about God being within, around and beyond all things. The text goes on to talk about how the Holy Spirit will enlighten and enable all those who seek to be on the Way of God. The term Holy Spirit is here given as 'the incessantly working spirit'.

We then come to yet another question from Simon Peter who asks how a positive experience such as joy can exist in one who has achieved a state of non-action – the state in which you do not seek to control. This is the state which Jesus has just declared is the one necessary if true Rest and Joy are to be found. Jesus uses a lovely analogy:

> It might be compared to a lonely uninhabited mountain, full of all sorts of woods and trees, which have numerous leaves and branches spreading in all directions, giving shade and shelter. Although this mountain and its forests do not invite birds and beasts to come, yet all kinds of birds and beasts will seek this mountain and the forests and will come and settle there, of their own accord.

Jesus then proceeds to say that this teaching is unique and mysterious and that no other faith can compare. Its effects are not just beneficial to the listener, but to those who genuinely believe, the benefits of the mysterious Rest and Joy will be extended also to their ancestors. Here the Chinese belief in ancestors is given a place and a meaning, but within a Christian framework.

He talks of how the actions of those who have gone before us condition us, both by their good deeds and by their bad. But the teaching which Jesus is bringing can break us free from this, and its effects reverberate back into time as well as into our own lives and into the lives of those yet to come.

We then come to the description of the purpose of Jesus Christ's coming on earth. It is a beautiful piece and I give it in full.

> The Unique Lord, the Messiah said, 'Truly, truly I say to you, it is exactly as you say. For instance, it [the teachings] can be compared to the Precious Mountain. Its jade forests and pearl fruits, translucent and shining, sweet tasting and beautifully perfumed, can cure a person of hunger and thirst and heal all ills.
>
> There was a sick man who heard of this mountain. Day and

night he longed to reach this mountain and the thought never left him.

But, sadly, the way was far and the mountain very high and steep. The sick man was also a hunchback and was too feeble to climb such a mountain. In vain did he try to fulfil his dream. He simply could not undertake it. But he had a near relation who was both wise and sincere. This man set up scaling ladders and had steps cut into the mountain and with others he pushed and pulled the sick man up the mountain until he reached the summit. Immediately, the sick man's illness was cured.

Know this, Simon Peter, that the people coming to this mountain of true teachings were for a long time confused and in misery because they were burdened by their worldly passions. They had heard of the truth and knew it could lead them to the Way of Rest and Joy – to the Mountain of Rest and Joy. They tried to reach the mountain and to scale it, but in vain, for love and faith had almost died within them.

Thereupon, the Almighty Lord made himself known. He came as the near relative of the people and taught them with such skill and sincerity that they understood that he was both the scaling ladder and the stone steps by means of which they could understand the True Way and rid themselves of their burdens of confusion for ever.'

So here is Jesus, the 'near relative' and the 'scaling ladder and stone steps', by which all life is saved. I find this a touching and moving analogy, in which nothing is lost of the purpose or meaning of the incarnation. This is the particular skill of Ching-ching the priest. He is able to find new and appropriate images and models by which the eternal truths of the Christian faith can be conveyed to an audience for whom talk of a shepherd and his sheep, or a fisherman and his nets would be unimpressive and fail to convey the notion of salvation wrought through one man's actions and life. Just as the Celts, tens of thousands of miles away saw no problem in incorporating models and images from their former faith, so Ching-ching the Nestorian saw no problem in recasting the gospel into Chinese literary and religious imagery.

After this come the Ten Ways of Contemplation. Briefly summarized, for they go on at some length, they are:

1.   This body lasts only so long and then is gone. All that lives, dies.

2.   We all eventually have to be separated from those we love, by death.

3.   While some are wealthy and others poor, all such wealth is meaningless at death (see the gospel story about storing up your treasures on earth).

4.   All who are selfish and evil in this life will find that this has brought them nothing but suffering.

5.   We all put our energies into accumulating comforts, but none of these will be of use in the end.

6.   We are all held in thrall by sexual passions but these only serve to tie us even more into trouble and suffering.

7.   All human beings deaden their minds and bodies by the use of drink, drugs and pleasure seeking, until eventually we cannot tell right from wrong.

8.   We exist in this world as if we were here to amuse ourselves. This wastes our time and saps our mental powers.

9.   We are all attracted to false teachings which draw us away from acting justly and truly.

10.   Many who claim to have found the true path are simply seeking glory for themselves.

From these Ten Ways of Contemplation, Jesus then says that you can progress to the Four States of the Victorious Law. Again I will summarize them:

1.   Non-desire. Do not give in to the lure of desire which allows you to be overcome by emotions.

2.   Non-action or selflessness. Do nothing externally that is at variance with your inner self. This means no action will be done which goes against that which is true. There should be no action just for the sake of action or for gratification of the self.

3.   Non-virtue. Likewise, do not do things just so people will talk favourably about you and your virtue. Do things because they are right, even if no-one notices them or praises you.

4.   Non-demonstration. Be who you are, not what others want and you will have an immense effect, but not by showing off. Jesus says, 'There is nothing that the mirror does not reflect accurately, yet the mirror is unaware of this. We therefore, should behave likewise.'

Jesus then goes on to say that these teachings are like the armour a soldier puts on in order to go to war, or the seaworthy ship that you need to cross the ocean.

> Only the Law Books of the Supremely Victorious Law of this Shining Teaching can give life to the dead and save all people from the sea of life and death and thus lead them to the other shore of existence, full of the precious scent of Rest and Joy . . . Only the Law Books of the Supremely Victorious Law of this Shining Teaching will restore the true mind and life of all living beings, while also making all the miseries of sin vanish for ever.

These texts are heavily influenced by Buddhism and it is clear that Ching-ching is now taking language and ideas from Buddhism and seeing what Christian insights they might have and what they can contribute to giving greater depth of understanding to the Chinese of Christian beliefs, whereas earlier he was looking for Chinese terms to be used to express Christian teachings.

Finally Jesus gives his Great Commission as told at the end of Matthew's gospel.

> Go therefore into the world my disciples and all you who have heard my doctrines. Go and do as I have taught you in this Sutra.

The Sutra ends thus, using an old Chinese proverb:

> Simon Peter rose and with great respect asked him to speak further. But the Messiah replied to him saying, 'Ask no more. My preaching may be compared to a good well which always gives forth

water. But if you are just recovering from an illness, no matter how much water is available, you should only drink a little, for otherwise you will be ill again. Therefore I had better not preach any more at the moment.

Listening to these words all those present were filled with happiness and joy. Saluting the Messiah most respectfully, they all retired and acted upon the orders of the Lord.

Here ends the Sutra of the utmost Pure and Serene Rest and Joy.

THE LEGACY OF THE CHINESE NESTORIANS

I believe that the Nestorian church in China made a most significant and interesting attempt to translate the gospel, not just into another language, but into another culture and belief system. They were often despised by the nineteenth- and early twentieth-century Protestant missionaries to China. I believe the missionaries were wrong to do so, and that the rejection of the Nestorians' attempts at acculturation perhaps accounts for the fact that despite their efforts – the greatest missionary venture in history – China by 1949 was still less than one per cent Christian.

I believe that the Nestorians can jolt us into seeing how culture-bound our version of the truth of God incarnate in humanity is. They can also challenge us to try and express the gospel in terms of the cultures and beliefs which surround us today, and to do so with integrity but not with dogmatism. After all, the Nestorian church obviously respected Ching-ching, for it not only gave him the honour of composing the Nestorian Stone, but 200 years after his death, he was still known and honoured by his church. His works are not those of a maverick, but of a deeply loved father of the church – a father who has gone unhonoured for too long.

Of Nestorian Christianity in China today, virtually nothing remains. There is the stone, the stone crosses which depict the cross arising from the lotus and which adorned the tombs of Christians of the eighth–eleventh centuries. But of the faith itself, there is nothing, except the goddess Kuan Yin. So, did

Nestorian Christianity fail? At one level, yes. When the Nestorians became closely tied in with the power structures of the
Mongolian tribes and when they rode to conquest amongst the
hordes of Genghis Khan, they made a major shift in their
position. Instead of being the yeast fermenting away within the
culture of the peoples of China, Tibet or Mongolia, they trod
the same path as the faith did in the late Roman Empire. They
aligned themselves with the secular power of the day.

For a brief while, it looked as if a second vast Christian
empire would arise to the east of the Roman/Byzantine Empire.
But instead, Islam won. Having placed their future in the scales
and having lost, the Nestorians began to decline for they were
now seen as opponents. In China, they came to be associated
with the hated rule of the Yuan dynasty – the Mongol. As such,
when the Mongols where thrown out, the remnants of Nestorian Christianity went with them. Further west into Afghanistan
and Persia, the conversion of most of the tribes to Islam put the
Christians on the defensive and they began to lose numbers.
Finally, the genocidal attacks of Tamerlane in the early fifteenth
century destroyed almost all that remained of the culture and
lifestyle of this once great, minority, missionary church.

For me, it is the church in China which marks the high point
of Nestorian Christianity. From the pen of such missionaries as
Ching-ching we see how Christianity can be totally different in
its style, imagery and symbolism from the particular ways we
have grown accustomed to hearing it and believing it to be. Yet
we can also see that the fundamental insights about the love of
the creator for all life, shown in the incarnation, passion, teachings and resurrection of Christ, are able to be communicated
just as powerfully as the Greek version, or the legalistic Latin or
the Germanic nationalistic versions have been. Perhaps because
it is not associated with the failures of those cultures, it may
even be able to speak more clearly and more challengingly to
us, precisely because it is not familiar. In the Nestorian church in
general, as a largely non-imperialistic, non-state church, we can
see what Christianity can be like if it is not part of the power-
play and traumas of a Christendom. In the efforts of the Chinese
Nestorians, we can see the gospel taken out of the linguistic and

conceptual framework of the West and placed freely and with integrity into a totally different context. Such insights show that Christianity is too powerful to be contained by any culture, language or belief system.

5

Telling New Stories of Christianity

So what sort of stories about Christ and the faith are being told today? In looking back over the varied histories of Christianity in different parts of the world, I have tried to show that it is a pluralist faith within itself. This is as true today as it ever was.

The face of Christianity has changed dramatically in the last few decades. Those who experienced it as children and rejected it will in many cases find that what they rejected has itself been rejected by the Church or by significant sections of it. I want to start by looking at some of the changes that have taken place within Christianity, and at the forces which have brought about these changes.

THE MONSTROUS REGIMENT OF WOMEN

In the early nineties, a bizarre ritual took place in one of the main Anglican theological colleges in Cambridge. One evening, three people, one a priest, the other two students, emerged in full ceremonial regalia from the chapel of the college. Processing through the college, they arrived at the central courtyard. There they ceremonially burned a book of prayers and reflections by a leading feminist theologian and liturgist.

At one level this could be seen as the sort of excessive action typical of students. At another level, it is a very disturbing image. For the conflict between traditional beliefs and attitudes about women and the call for them to have a full place within the Church has profound consequences for Christianity.

The impetus for the feminist challenge to traditional Christianity did not originate within the Church. It came from outside. It came as women, especially women writers and academics, began to dissect the patriarchal nature of Western society – indeed, of most societies. Naturally a faith which has the Father and the Son as key words and concepts is going to attract some attention. This is exactly what happened, with women outside the faith attacking the outspoken patriarchal and often anti-feminine bias of the Church. In their turn, certain eminent women theologians within the Church began to ask very fundamental questions about Christianity in the light not just of the particular critiques of Christianity by women, but also of the wider philosophical, linguistic and socio-political issues raised by the women's movement.

These challenges have led many women to give up on Christianity altogether. Mary Daly and Daphne Hampson are perhaps the best known of these. Both theologians, they have now declared that they can no longer believe in Christianity. Indeed, they would now say that Christianity is in itself one of the major obstacles to women achieving any sort of equality or quality of life. They find it so inherently and irredeemably sexist and patriarchal as to be beyond redeeming. Mary Daly says for instance:

> The biblical and popular image of God as a great patriarch in heaven, rewarding and punishing according to his mysterious and seemingly arbitrary will, has dominated the imagination of millions over thousands of years. The symbol of the Father God, spawned in the human imagination and sustained as plausible by patriarchy, has in turn rendered service to this type of society by making its mechanism for the oppression of women appear right and fitting. If God in 'his' heaven is a father ruling 'his' people, then it is in the 'nature' of things and according to divine plan and the order of the universe that society be male-dominated.
>
> As the Women's Movement begins to have its effect upon the fabric of society, transforming it from patriarchy into something that never existed before, into a diarchal situation that is radically

new, it can become the greatest single challenge to the major religions of the world, Western and Eastern – all of which are essentially sexist.

Ms. 3 (December 1974), pp. 58–9.

Daphne Hampson, lecturer in theology in Scotland, and now a 'post-Christian feminist' has since declared:

> It will be clear then that there is nothing intrinsically incompatible between being a feminist and conceiving of oneself as a religious person. Indeed, feminism may well allow us to develop our conceptualisation of God in helpful ways. There is, however, I believe, an incompatibility between being feminist and Christian. The clash is structural and relates to the nature of feminist and Christian thought.
>
> *Feminist Theology – A Reader*, edited by Ann Loades, SPCK, 1990, p.225.

For those who stay within the churches and grapple with these issues, there have come to be two key battles around which all the questions and conflicts swirl. Can God be considered as Mother and can women be ordained as priests.

I suspect that in thirty or forty years' time, we shall be astonished that these issues were a cause of conflict. Just as we now look back on the debate about slavery within the churches in the nineteenth century and are amazed that any Christians could have opposed the ending of slavery, so I imagine we shall review this episode in our religious conceptual history in the same way. This is perhaps a sign of how fast and far Christianity has moved in response to the feminist critique. But the severity with which the battles have been fought shows that it is not just a case of readjusting certain phrases or actions. Feminism is asking very central questions about authority and power within the Church as well as about the nature of the divine and our relationship to it.

When the three students in Cambridge carried out their ritual, they were manifesting what many would see as a deep-seated fear of women – misogyny – within the Church. The antagonism to any imagery or language about God which

includes the feminine is very entrenched. Scholars and theologians have explored some of the roots of this. The Old
Testament certainly depicts a struggle for identity between the
Israelites and the fertility religions of Palestine. The question of
whether Judaism suppressed an older and equally valid interpretation of God as female is one which exercises many minds. The
conspiracy theory about the major world religions is that they
are all guilty of the suppression and then repression of the
Goddess – an older, more venerable tradition of worship of the
female, which the patriarchal major world religions deliberately
usurped and then silenced.

Claims that traces of this older view can be found in the Bible
have created considerable debate. For instance, Dr Phyllis Trible
of Union Theological Seminary, New York, traces remnants of
female deity language within the Old Testament. An example is
Deuteronomy 32: 18: 'You were unmindful of the Rock that
begot you and you forgot the God who gave you birth.' The
Hebrew verb actually has only one meaning, that of the pains
and struggles of a woman in labour. Moreover, in Hosea 11,
God speaks as a mother does about rearing her children, Israel
and Judah. Perhaps most intriguing of all is the plural 'us' in
Genesis 1: 26: 'God said "Let us make humanity in our image, in
the likeness of ourselves".' Behind the patriarchal façade of the
Old Testament therefore some claim there lies the hazy shape
of belief in God as both father and mother – probably along the
lines of the heavens as father and earth as mother. Certainly this
would accord with virtually all evidence of the religious beliefs
of the ancient Middle East.

Coming to the figure of Jesus, the question becomes one of
what Jesus' attitude was towards women and whether the early
Church was guilty of suppressing a tradition of the equality,
possibly even the superiority of women within the ranks of his
disciples. Certainly there is strong evidence that Jesus treated
women more as equals than would be normal for a man of that
time. The gospels also show that women played a key role in
his group of followers. Take for example his encounter with the
woman taken in adultery (John 8: 1–11), the fact that he first
revealed himself to a woman after his resurrection and the fact

that the resurrection itself was revealed by the angels at the tomb to women disciples.

Elaine Pagels, in her studies of the recently discovered gnostic gospels, shows that there was a tradition which not only addressed God as both father and mother, but also defended the right of Mary Magdalene to be considered as an authority amongst the disciples, for she was appointed by Jesus himself. One incident in particular illustrates the tensions believed to have existed even at the start of the life of the Church. Mary has just had a vision of the risen Christ who has spoken to her. The teachings thus revealed are spurned by Andrew and most of the other disciples. Peter in particular disagrees:

> Mary wept and said to Peter, 'My brother Peter, what do you think? Do you think I thought this up myself in my heart? Do you think I am lying about the Saviour?' Levi answered and said to Peter, 'Peter, you have always been hot-tempered. If the Saviour made her worthy, who are you to reject her?'
>
> (*The Gnostic Gospels* by Elaine Pagels, first published 1979, this edition, Penguin, 1990, p. 43).

The gnostic gospels were of course excluded from the canon of the New Testament in the fourth century. It is claimed, probably with some justification, that one test of orthodoxy for inclusion of writings within the canon, was whether they agreed with the patriarchal development of the Church and of Christian theology.

In recent years, this patriarchal hold on our beliefs as Christians has been challenged in a simple yet effective way. The language we use to address or describe God has been altered. When I was a child, indeed when I was a student radical, I never noticed the language of the Bible or prayers or hymns. When someone first started talking about sexist language within the Church, I was not sure I agreed with them. In contrast, my daughter Elizabeth, from the age of six onwards objected to the exclusive nature of much language within traditional and even modern church services. I recall very clearly her asking me where the woman was in the trinity. Elizabeth is not a great radical or rebel. Far from it. She has a great sense of responsibility and quite a respect for authority. She doesn't really like it if our vicar is away from our church – it's not proper. But she bristles at sexist language and feels excluded by it.

I now find that I have exactly the same response. I find exclusive language, talk of Christ dying 'for all men' or praying that God will bestow peace 'on all men' highly offensive. For my wife, the insistence of the Church of England, on using exclusive language while claiming that it is really inclusive, is so offensive that she finds it virtually impossible to worship using conventional prayer books or hymns.

But a great shift has taken place, and I do not think it is a superficial one. I think it is about the rediscovery of a lost or hidden dimension of our relationship with God the creator, with creation and with each other. The feminine side of creation is crucial to a proper understanding of God as lover of all creation, all life. But it is also deeply threatening to those whose own self-image is tied up with patriarchy. Mary Daly points out in her disturbing book *Gyn-ecology* that it is not only men whose identity has been tied firmly to a patriarchal system. Some of the stoutest defenders of patriarchy are those women whose lives have been shaped by subservience to such a model.

The 'crime' of the theologian whose book was burnt in Cambridge, Janet Morley, was that she addressed God as Mother. The reaction by the priest and students shows how profoundly such a statement challenges values and beliefs. Yet theology and indeed the Church has always maintained that all metaphors such as God the Father, the Good Shepherd and so forth, are but pale imitations, mere hints at the real nature of God, which is beyond the capacity of human language to express or even to experience. The claim of those defending patriarchy within the churches is that the metaphor of God as Father is more than just a metaphor. It is in fact an expression of the nature of God. God is, for them, male and to suggest that he is not, is to deny the very essence of what God is.

Turning to the issue of the ordination of women, we can see how some of this general concern about the nature of God is expressed in a particular case. The issue of whether women can or cannot be ordained is only really an issue for those churches which believe in apostolic succession — the belief that the hierarchy of the church — bishops, priests, deacons and so forth — has come down from Christ and represents a divine order. Furthermore, the right of succession, the gift of the priesthood, has been handed down directly from the apostles through the centuries to our day. The laying on of hands at an ordination links the new priest in a direct unbroken line to the laying on of hands by the apostles to their first followers. This is what apostolic succession means: that the priest is a direct descendant of the apostles. This doctrine takes us into the question of authority and maleness.

Those who oppose the ordination of women say that if Christ had wanted women to be priests, he would have chosen women to be amongst his twelve disciples. Furthermore, they claim that when the priest stands at the altar, he represents Christ as the priest of all life. Therefore, they argue, the priest must be like the first apostles, a man. But if this is the case, surely one should not just stop at the gender of the apostles. Should one not also have priests who are circumcized, Jewish and basically working class?

What Christ was actually doing when he chose his twelve apostles is not clear. We need to remember that Jesus also appointed a group of seventy-two disciples whom he person-ally sent out to carry his message from village to village. Feminist critics of the 'Jesus only chose men', school of argu-ment point out that women feature prominently amongst the disciples, and that in the earliest churches they seem to have had equality with men. Paul himself refers to women such as Phoebe as a deacon, Junia as an apostle, and Prisca as a co-worker.

When pressed, many opponents of the ordination of women admit that there really is no logical, theological or even Biblical reason why they should not be ordained, but they feel a deep unease about it. When pressed even further, this unease is revealed as having very little if anything to do with the Chris-tian faith. It is rooted in a fear of women and in a hankering for a Church which remains the same. It is also fear of opening the flood gates. Once you accept that the Church has been labour-ing under a false understanding of the gospel, born more of the culture of patriarchy than of the truth of the gospel, you begin to look equally critically at other aspects of the traditional expression of the faith as we have received it. For there is no doubt that once you admit the validity of much of the feminist critique of conventional Christianity, you have to admit that much else in the Church may be culturally defined rather than derived from the gospel. If you then accept that the critique is valid in terms of revealing the clouding or cloaking of the heart of the Christian message with baggage which is unnecessary and even harmful to the gospel, then you have to face the possibility that there are other aspects to the Church's presentation of Christ's message which may also be compromised or hide the revelation of God in Christ.

While there are many other issues which are forcing the Christian faith to retell its story, I believe that it is the encounter with feminism which is providing the most profound challenge to contemporary Christianity and to its own self-understanding. Feminism raises more sharply and more brutally than any other issue the question of whether the Christian faith can abandon language and imagery, even that which appears in its sacred literature, the Bible, in order to express anew the saving grace of the faith and the meaning of God for all life. More intensely than in any other debate, feminism is asking the faithful to let go of images which are no longer useful and which may indeed have been very damaging. Whether, as Daphne Hampson concludes, it is impossible to be a Christian and a feminist, or whether feminism can help us rediscover the true meaning of God and of ourselves, this exploration is changing the face and language of Christianity in just as profound a way as Chingching in China changed the face and language of his understanding of Christianity in order to speak to and learn from the cultures of ancient China.

WHOSE CULTURE, WHOSE FAITH?

I was discussing our mutual Christian faith with some colleagues in Kenya recently. My friends, Obed, Peter, John and

Mary, were talking about work we were doing together on incorporating traditional African religious ideas into the framework of Christian educational materials. The conversation turned to names. Shaking their heads, they told me of one colleague who insisted on using only his African name, Ng'ang'a. As the discussion continued, I realized something which had never struck me before. All my Christian friends thought that in order to be a Christian, you had to discard your African name at baptism (which often comes in the teens or twenties) and take on a Christian name — that is a Western, biblical or saint's name. As this seemed to be rather a drastic symbol of the rejection of African tradition, I began to question it. Was it really necessary? Their answer was that without a 'Christian' name, how could one be a Christian?

To this I replied that my own name, whilst it was that of a saint, in fact meant 'soldier of Mars', and had only become Christian because a pagan soldier called Martin had been converted. I also mentioned that my father's name, Derek, was not a saint's name, nor was my sister Sheila's. These were names which the family liked and which originated in our culture's pre-Christian past.

A look of total astonishment spread over the faces of my colleagues. They had thought that all Christians were called by names taken from the saints or from the Bible. Indeed, it was obvious to them that a sign of having become a Christian was the adoption of a Western, 'Christian' name. As we began to explore this issue, we realized what a sad and destructive thing had been done to African self-identity within the Church by this habit. I was able to point to other branches of Christianity — ancient ones at that — where the pre-Christian names continued to be used by those who were converted to the faith and even by those born into it. We looked at the names of early Christians and saw that many saints' names clearly showed that they came from the pre-Christian culture and had simply become Christian because of association, not because there was anything quintessentially 'Christian' about them. Saints such as Dionysius, Hormidz and Thorlac clearly show the evidence of Greek, Zoroastrian and Norse mythology in their names. Yet this did prevent them from becoming part of the breadth of 'Christian' names.

The imposition of one cultural model of Christianity – the Western model – has been the cause of immense problems in recent years. As many countries in Africa, Asia and South America received their ·Christian faith via the priests and missionaries who rode the tide of colonialism and conquest, these churches and Christians in a post-colonial era have had to do some heavy soul-searching. Core questions are: is Christianity irredeemably tarnished by its links with colonialism? Do we have to accept the baggage of Western theology in order to be Christians? Can we develop an expression of Christianity which uses local, traditional beliefs and imagery? What is the relationship between this new faith and the older culture and faith which has so profoundly shaped us?

The struggle to find an expression of Christianity which takes account of indigenous culture has taken two main forms. The first is through radical reassessments within existing, Western-derived, denominations. The second has been through the emergence of indigenous churches which owe nothing to the West.

Professor Chung Hyun-kyung's Vision

In 1991, the World Council of Churches (WCC) held its seven-yearly general assembly in Canberra, Australia. The WCC is the largest body representing the Protestant and Orthodox churches around the world. It has long been at the centre of the more radical and challenging expressions of Christianity. It represents very clearly within its 300-plus member churches, the fact that Christianity is the faith of the poor and marginalized of the world. It has often been the only body capable of getting the older, Western denominations to listen properly to the voices and stories coming from the churches of the poor two-thirds of the world.

The Canberra assembly was remarkable for the dramatic – in every sense of the word – presentation by a young theologian from South Korea, Chung Hyun-kyung. Her presentation on the theme of the Holy Spirit — 'Come Holy Spirit, Renew the Whole Creation' — created such a storm that an additional session had to be held to answer charges of heresy. Chung, a Presbyterian, sought to contextualize her understanding of the Holy Spirit by drawing upon deep roots and beliefs within her own faith, her country's traditional culture, and other sources, usually seen as, at the least, 'unchristian'. The following account of her presentation comes from the WCC's own magazine *One World* No. 164, March/April 1991.

In a dramatic entry on to the plenary stage, accompanied by 16 young Australian Koreans, Chung began by joining with two Aboriginal dancers to invoke the spirits of victims of tragic death.

The roster included biblical characters — Hagar, Uriah, the young boys killed by Herod; historical figures named and unnamed — Joan of Arc, indigenous people killed during the colonial period, Jews murdered in Nazi gas chambers, and more contemporary victims.

Among the latter she called on the spirits of those who died at Bhopal and Chernobyl, of 'people smashed by tanks in Kwangju, Tiananmen Square and Lithuania,' of 'Earth, Air and Water, raped and tortured and exploited by human greed for money' and of 'soldiers, civilians and sea-creatures now dying in the bloody war in the Gulf.'

Following her call to these spirits, she burned the list and let the ashes drift upwards.

If the intercession 'Come Holy Spirit' means 'O God, we messed up again, come and fix up all our problems,' said Chung, it is an infantile prayer.

'I know that I no longer believe in an omnipotent, macho, warrior God who rescues all good guys and punishes all bad guys. Rather, I rely on the compassionate God who weeps with us for life in the midst of cruel destruction of life.'

If we are 'to survive on this dying planet' she said, three changes are needed. One is from 'anthropocentrism' to 'life-centrism.' In contrast to traditional Christian theology and Western thinking, she said, 'we have to reread the Bible from the perspective of birds, water, air, trees and mountains, the most wretched of the earth in our time'.

A second change is from 'dualism' to 'interconnection.' When dualism came into the world, she said, 'we began to objectify "others" as separate from ourselves,' making them 'objects one can control as one likes'.

In contrast, she said, is the traditional Northeast Asia understanding of the life energy, ki, which 'thrives in the harmonious interconnections among sky, earth and people'.

Finally is the change from a 'culture of death' to a 'culture of life'.

Bringing together these three changes of orientation, she then sketched her own image of the Holy Spirit, derived not from her 'academic training as a systematic theologian but from my gut feeling deep in my people's collective unconsciouness that comes from thousands of years of spirituality'.

The image, she said 'comes from the image of Kwan In [the Kuan-yin of Chapter 4]. She is venerated as the Goddess of compassion and wisdom by East Asian women's popular religiosity . . .' Her compassion for all suffering living beings makes her stay in this world, enabling other living beings to achieve enlightenment. Her compassionate wisdom heals all forms of life and empowers them to swim to the shore of Nirvana . . . Perhaps this might be the feminine image of the Christ who is first born among us, one who goes before and brings others with her.'

As can be imagined, Chung's presentation raised many hackles amongst the more conventional Christians present. But what was she doing that was really different from the absorption of pre-Christian deities into the ranks of the saints in early Christianity. What she was doing was taking the truth of Jesus Christ and of the love and compassion of God and setting it within as broad a context as possible. She was looking at what happens when you take a belief, such as the Christian one of the Holy Spirit, as that which brings life and light to all life, or of God as the God of all history not just Jewish and Christian history, and apply it to cultures which have not traditionally been Christian. The results mean we have to conceive of God's purpose and God's involvement with life on a scale which stretches and then breaks the usual models we have developed.

From the discovery that African traditional names can be used as names for Christians to the all-embracing theology of Chung, the churches of Africa, Asia and Latin America are waking up to the fact that they do not have to see the world, themselves or God through the narrow perspectives of language, imagery and ritual developed from the Graeco-Hebrew world perspective.

Indigenous Churches

The second way in which the Christians of the poor 'two-thirds' world are expressing themselves is through indigenous churches — churches which have arisen spontaneously within particular cultures, especially those of Africa. They have no direct, historical links with the older Western denominations, but represent an expression of Christianity amongst people who have often had bad experiences with Western culture, or no links with the West at all.

Not all these new manifestations remain recognizably Christian. The Unification Church of the Rev. Moon is one example. While derived from certain aspects of Christianity, it has developed a theology of the divinity of Rev. Moon and his family which places it firmly outside the bounds of Christianity. In other parts of the world, personality cults with a Christian tinge are also to be found. But there are many more movements which are identifiably Christian and yet have no links with traditional Christianity. These indigenous churches offer a fascinating model of how the truths of Christianity can be experienced without the dogma, doctrines or apparatus of conventional Christianity, though they soon form their own dogmas and traditions, as is the wont of all human institutions!

One example of a 'successful' indigenous church is the Kimbanguists of Zaire. The official title of this church is the Church of Jesus Christ on Earth through the Prophet Simon Kimbangu. Its origins lie with a young man who was a member of a Baptist congregation, Simon Kimbangu, who was born in 1889. In 1918, Simon began to hear Christ calling him. 'I am the Christ', the voice said. 'My servants are unfaithful, I have chosen you to witness and convert your brothers.'

Simon kept this revelation to himself and wrestled with it.

Then in 1921, he felt called to visit a market town and to heal a woman in the name of Christ. More healings followed, though Simon seems to have resisted the call to heal. Soon he was surrounded by a vast crowd and his miracles were reported far and wide. The Kimbanguist church sees this period – a few months in 1921 – as comparable to the effects of the first Pentecost on the disciples. So strong is their sense that what could happen in Palestine could also happen in the Belgian Congo (as it then was) that they actually see the gift of the Holy Spirit as having been brought to them by Simon Kimbangu. Hence the title of the Church which stresses his central role, but it is a role which places Simon under the aegis of the trinity, not, as so often happens with charismatic figures in new movements, on a par with it.

The Belgian colonial authorities were scared by what they saw happening: a popular, indigenous form of Christianity arising that was beyond their control. In late 1921, a Belgian colonial officer by the name of Morel was sent to investigate the movement. His report captures perfectly what the colonial authorities most feared about indigenous churches.

Kimbangu wants to found a religion which reflects the mentality of the Africans, a religion which contains the fundamentals of Protestantism, mixed up with the practices of witchcraft . . . Everyone can see that the European religions have been petrified by abstractions and do not correspond to the mentality of the Africans who are longing for tangible facts and protection from demons. The religion of Kimbangu suits them because it is supported by tangible facts . . . Therefore it is necessary to fight Kimbangu. His tendency is pan-African. Natives will say: 'We have found a God of the blacks, a religion which corresponds to the Africans'

(Quoted in *Pentecost between Black and White*, by Walter Hollenweger, Christian Journal Ltd, Belfast, 1974.)

Kimbangu was captured, and tried and condemned to death. This sentence was commuted to life imprisonment and he spent the last thirty years of his life in prison, dying in 1951. His followers were heavily persecuted and over 100,000 of them were exiled during this same period. This simply had the effect of assisting the spread of his teachings.

In 1960, the Kimbanguists, now officially permitted to practise their faith, issued a list of their ethics and teachings. These include respect for the authorities and abstention from strong drinks, drugs, tobacco, dancing and swimmimg naked, and sleeping naked. They were forbidden to practise witchcraft or eat pork or monkey, and were required always to seek peaceful means of resolving disputes.

The Kimbanguists have spread widely. In Zaire itself, they have some five million members, and there are also sizeable communities in Congo, Angola, Zambia, Gabon, the Central African Republic, Burundi, Kenya, France, Belgium and Portugal.

The Church has made an impressive contribution to social-action Christianity, with an extensive educational, medical and social services programme. The Church has taken a principled stance against the advances of both capitalism and communism, practising instead a community-based co-operative model for its own finances and structures. Its very strong emphasis on the Holy Spirit means that it is constantly seeking the coming of the Spirit upon people in ways which lead them to repentance and action. Through its membership of the World Council of Churches, it has shown that it is clearly trinitarian in teaching and that it considers itself but a part of the wider Church. This is in distinction to what happens in many new churches, which cast aside the rest of Christianity as irredeemably damned, and state their path as being the only true one.

The church leadership is hereditary, and in the late fifties, the sons of Simon set about reorganizing the Church as it became legally possible to do so. The principle of hereditary leadership is a strong one in indigenous churches.

Since Simon Kimbangu's original mission in 1921, over 500 other indigenous churches have appeared, but none has achieved the success or the theological originality within orthodoxy of the Kimbanguists. The issue for such churches is always that of authority. By what authority does the church exist and by what authority does the leader make his or her decisions? In the case of the Kimbanguists, the Bible and the invocation of the guidance of the Holy Spirit are the key elements of their authority structure, tempered by their understanding of themselves as a church for Africa which is then part of the wider family of the Church.

THE POOR WORLD'S FAITH

As I said in Chapter 1, one fundamental change that has occurred in recent decades is demographic. For 500 years, until the middle of this century, Christianity was predominantly the faith of the West and of the powerful. Since the end of the Second World War, it has shifted to being a predominantly poor world faith. The majority of practising Christians are now living below the United Nations poverty level, have little access to conventional means of power and are amongst the groups most adversely affected by the living standards and behaviour of the West.

According to the *World Christian Encyclopedia*, in 1900 there were some 470 million Christians in the West (the USA, Canada, western Europe, Australia and New Zealand); with some eighty three million in what is now called the Third World. By the mid-eighties the figures had changed dramatically. There were around 557 million Christians in the West and 685 million in the Third World.

This shift has had enormous consequences for Christianity. It has led to a breakdown in some of the conventional alliances between the powerful élites of the world and Christianity. The most notable instance of this has been in Latin America. Thirty years ago, anyone surveying Latin America would have identified the Roman Catholic church as not only the sole church of any significance there, but also one of the main pillars upon which the élite – military, economic and social – rested. As such, the Roman Catholic church was seen by many reformers and revolutionaries as one of the biggest blocks, if not the biggest, to progress. It was assumed that the Church would continue to defend the interests of the ruling classes because its own leadership was drawn from just that group. Its land holdings, status, wealth and prestige were such that it did not seem capable of any change in its allegiances.

That has now changed in many of the Latin American countries. To start with the Roman Catholic church is no longer a cohesive body. In many countries, there is a real split between those who are of the old regime, and those who have opted to side with the poor and powerless. The Church itself is no longer a monolith upon which the rich can build their self-justifications. Instead it has become one of the fiercest critics of social, economic and political injustice, calling down upon itself the wrath of its former friends. In doing so, however, it has split into two factions: those who are willing to relate the gospel to social action and those who fear such a linkage.

The origins of this dramatic and totally unforeseen change in the Roman Catholic church in Latin America can be traced back to two events in the sixties. The first was the Second Vatican Council held from 1962 to 1965. This great gathering of over 2000 bishops from around the world liberated the Church from the dead weight of much unnecessary tradition and habit. In particular it elevated the native languages of the people to become the language of the Mass, replacing the Latin Mass. This gave a great boost to the acceptance of the ordinary people and their culture into the Church. Secondly it asked the religious orders, the nuns and monks, to go back to the teachings and principles of their founders. This had the effect of radicalizing many of these orders because, when the hagiographies had been discarded, their founders were, almost without exception, people whose lives showed a commitment to the poor and displaced.

Then, in 1968, the Latin American Bishops' Conference met at Medellin, Colombia. Here, in what was later to become the drug capital of the world, they produced an astonishingly powerful political document. In it they gave the Church's blessing to the concept of 'liberation' which carried with it all the connotations of the struggle for freedom and justice – including the notion of armed struggle against forces of oppression. It also gave its blessing to a remarkable movement just emerging which is known as *Comunidades eclesiales de base,* or in English, basic Christian communities. At Medellin, the bishops called for action on an array of social, political and economic issues and for study of the root causes of injustice within each of these areas. In doing so they made it imperative for Christianity to discover or create tools of social criticism. For many, this meant borrowing heavily from Marxist critiques of the social order. This has proved to be a difficult path to follow, for it raises many basic questions. For instance, how much of Marxist ideology can the Church absorb without losing its faith? Once a critique has been made, what can the Church do? What is the nature of the relationship between the Church and the State, and does it matter if the State is democratic or not? What sort of economy should Christians support and how?

Liberation Theology and Basic Christian Communities

In Latin America the two most important developments have been the growth of liberation theology and ultimately more important, the growth of the basic Christian communities. These communities have arisen from the growing sense of the commitment to the poor – what is often termed the 'option for the poor'. Rereading the Bible, priests and theologians have discovered that God sides with the poor against the powerful. The witness of the exodus, of the prophets and of Jesus himself is cited to back this stance. The necessity for it to be expressed forcefully as an actual option, a decision in favour of the poor has come about because for so long the Church has opted for the rich and powerful.

The basic Christian communities are not, as has sometimes been claimed, a lay initiative. The initiative almost always has come first from the clergy or from parish workers. It involves a move away from the church-building, priest-led and sacrament-based ministry understanding of Christian life, to a much more home-based, localized and participatory model where sacraments such as communion are but part of a wider version of Christian life. As such, these communities – some-

times scores of them within one parish — are able to explore the
integration between the everyday life of the local people and
the gospels. Central to this whole process is the belief that God
cares for and sides with the poor against the powerful. It has
meant a new exploration of the meaning and mandate that the
Church has received from such texts as the Magnificat. The
Magnificat is the Song of Mary when she meets her cousin
Elizabeth. Both women are pregnant, Mary carrying Jesus in her
womb and Elizabeth, John the Baptist. The song is a hymn of
praise. For centuries, the Magnificat has been sung and chanted
in church. In the basic Christian communities and in liberation
theology the words have taken on a much more forceful meaning.

> My soul proclaims the greatness of the Lord,
> my spirit rejoices in God my saviour;
> for he has looked with favour on his lowly servant:
> from this day all generations shall call me blessed;
> the Almighty has done great things for me:
> and holy is his name.
>
> He has mercy on those who fear him:
> in every generation.
>
> He has shown the strength of his arm:
> he has scattered the proud in their conceit.
>
> He has cast down the mighty from their thrones:
> and has lifted up the lowly.
>
> He has filled the hungry with good things:
> and the rich he has sent empty away.
> He has come to the help of his servant Israel:
> for he remembered his promise of mercy,
> the promise he made to our fathers:
> to Abraham and his children for ever.

Suddenly, in the late sixties, these words, along with so much in
the exodus story and the prophets, held a new meaning for
many priests in the Third World. But even more importantly,

the song spoke through the Church to ordinary people who saw that God cared for them and sided with them. It is this fundamental sense that the story of the Bible is their story which has led people to form these basic Christian communities and through the strength and self-respect that they have gained from such fellowship and study, to struggle against their circumstances. The Roman Catholic church in Latin America has rediscovered the power of the story of redemption, of liberation, which is the core narrative in the Bible.

Basic Christian communities do not just offer places of Christian fellowship, but also act as activist cells. Through prayer, Bible study, worship, teaching and action, these communities learn to interpret the world around them – social, economic, political and natural – through the eyes of the radical vision of what should be that the Bible presents. With the aid of social criticism and philosophical and practical tools from Marxism and other ideologies, the ordinary Christian is equipped to understand the forces at work within his or her community. Through the solidarity which the basic Christian community provides, they discover that they are not alone and that concerted action by a group can change things. Thus the community might tackle unjust wages in their area, pollution, economic hardship, corruption, or even the violence of dictatorships and of the military. It is from the analytical study, from faith in the God of change and through solidarity one with another, that the basic Christian communities have come to challenge and to change so much of the way their societies are run. This has not endeared them to the establishment, ecclesiastical or secular.

These basic Christian communities have become the centre of many actions for community improvement and even for insurrection against unjust systems. At one level they represent a movement not dissimilar to the early Methodist classes. These were groups of ordinary people – miners, factory workers and the like – who gathered together, outside the confines of the established Church, to study together. The effect of being treated seriously, the growth of self-respect and the willingness to see the Bible story as in some sense a mandate for action today, is very similar in the Methodists' early history. The roots of much of the early trade union movement in the UK lies in these Methodist classes and the sense of worth which they gave to ordinary workers.

The basic Christian communities often have strong links to organizations such as indigenous people's groups, popular movements fighting for democratic rights, trade unions and civil rights groups, all of whom are struggling for human rights and dignity. The links between the basic Christian communities and these more secular, political bodies have brought difficulties. The radical bishops of 1968 have been replaced over the years by more conservative people. Some of the bishops at the 1968 meeting were also unaware quite what they were unleashing, and have stepped back from their former position. Add to this the election of a very conservative if charismatic pope and you can see that reaction was bound to set in. This is now the case in many parts of Latin America. The hierarchy is unable to deny the validity of these communities, but it does express grave doubts about the sort of company they keep!

That said, the Roman Catholic church in Latin America at the end of the twentieth century is not the same as the Church of the fifties. A shift in allegiance has taken place. The ruling classes of Latin America can no longer assume that the Church will bless their every action. Instead, they must deal with a Church which manifests at least two different attitudes to the State. The first is the traditional status quo attitude – blessing presidents and armies and dining with business chiefs. The second is the stance of the radical priest or nun working with the poor and of the socially aware Christian workers and peasants who have been equipped with critical tools for changing society.

The model of the basic Christian communities has inspired imitations throughout the world. Some have worked, as in areas such as the Philippines or South Korea. Others have not – there are a few such bodies functioning in the UK, for instance. There is perhaps an irony here. For it seems to be that societies where the faith and the Bible have not been subject to secular criticism are more able to develop a radical Christian critique and engagement with secular society. Meanwhile those societies, such as the UK, where the faith has been weakened by secular critiques, seem unable to bring themselves to believe that the faith and the Bible really do have a message which the secular world needs to hear.

Fundamental to the basic Christian communities and their outlook is liberation theology. I find that while many outside the faith are unaware of many of the changes inside Christianity, most have heard of liberation theology, even if they don't know quite what it is! At its most simple, liberation theology says that the meaning of the incarnation, of Christ's life, ministry, death and resurrection, lies in freeing people from oppression and enabling them to become masters of their own history. Students of liberation theology have identified a number of core concepts and presuppositions which spell out this vision.

Firstly, salvation or liberation is part of the history of the whole world and of all people, not just the story of the 'saved', of the 'chosen people' or of the Church. Bearing in mind that liberation theology arises in the context of Roman Catholic dominance, this is a very significant development. Until the Second Vatican Council, the Church's teaching was simple. There was no possibility of salvation outside the Roman Catholic church. This meant that the rest of life, social structures, other Christian denominations, other faiths, ideologies or world stances were incapable of any redeeming or liberating power. They simply were not part of God's purpose in salvation. Thus all history other than that of the Bible or the Church itself, was irrelevant. At the Second Vatican Council, this rigid and absolute point of view was modified. God was at work outside the Roman Catholic church. In Latin America this was understood to mean that all human activity, all movements for justice and equality, were capable of inclusion in God's saving, liberating work. The Church was thus freed to examine the world through the eyes of Christ's compassion and anger rather than to condemn it for not accepting Christ. From this it became possible for Marxist ideas to be seen as valid tools for Christians to use, within an overall Christian perspective. Even more importantly, it meant that participation in the struggles of the world was incorporated as part of the process of salvation, rather than seen as a distraction from it.

Secondly, liberation theology is concerned with practical actions – praxis – not just theory. Liberation theology argues that it is in the doing, not just the saying, that the Church should be judged. The word praxis is used to emphasize the Marxist idea of the transition from philosophers talking about problems to the people doing something about them. An interesting example of what this means theologically is the issue of conflict. Traditionally the Church has stressed harmony and peace as being the desired goal of Christian life – indeed of life itself. However, it has been very bad at actually saying how we get from our conflict-ridden world to the desired state of peace and harmony. Liberation theology stresses that conflict is in fact normative and that through confronting conflict – as Christ did upon the cross – theology or the Church is confronting reality and helping to lay some foundation stones upon which a more just society can be built. The emphasis on justice means that peace is often not a priority, for in order to have justice, you will have to struggle, and often to suffer.

Arising from this is the third insight, that truth is to be found through action and experience, not through absolute unaltering propositions. Theology, say the liberation theologians, arises not from the study of dusty books or from sitting through lectures, but from experiencing life and its struggles. Again, this is rooted in the incarnation. God speaks to us about his very nature and the nature of love, not so much through discourses or teachings as through history and through encounters with conflict. It is through historical, cultural and social encounters – such as the freeing of the Hebrew slaves from Egypt and the traumas of the exodus; the fall of Jerusalem to the Babylonians and the experience of exile and the consequent new understandings of God's purpose for the Jews; and the life and passion of Christ – that God reveals truth to us – truth about who we are, why God loves us and what we are called to be. These are the truths encountered in action and thus in history, and it is only by running the risk of new encounters, new understandings of the truth, that Christians can live and grow.

From this flows the fourth consideration, namely that truth is not objective. If it is discovered through history and action, then it is also encountered in specific situations and these will mark and shape our understanding of it. Any theology, including liberation, arises from a particular culture and background. As such it is always partisan because of its context and origin. Thus there can be no overall truth which functions regardless of context. All truth is experienced as subjective and any claim to objectivity is in fact the attempt of one group to assert its particular understanding at the expense of others.

Now a problem arises, for liberation theology does in fact do just that. It claims that the preference for the poor is an absolute, revealed in the particular actions of God in the Bible and in history. It is a danger within liberation theology which at times means we should talk more of a liberation *ideology* than of a liberation *theology*. But it is always the case that when new movements arise to confront past systems, they tend to overstate their case.

Finally, great emphasis is placed upon the priests' and the Church's identification with the poor. It is part of the creed of liberation theology that you cannot be a liberation theologian unless you have personally identified with the poor and oppressed. However, this is a controversial claim. While the original theologians did indeed arrive at their conclusions through political and social action, the same cannot be claimed for all those who have followed. Indeed, in part, liberation theology has suffered from being hijacked by boring academics who claim to identify with the poor while continuing to enjoy all the privileges of their academic posts and the perks of international conferences *about* identifying with the poor.

In the mid-eighties I visited a large number of churches and church organizations around the world. Many of them espoused liberation theology and had all the right catchphrases; more than half of them were living a lie. I was deeply disillusioned by this and the extent to which liberation theology's original insights have been taken over, packaged and retailed by the academic world is still to me a scandal. Having said that, I did and do meet people whose lives express what liberation theology tries to explain. They are inspired by liberation theology, but mostly by the encounter with God in action – one of its core principles – rather than through reading the latest heavy tome on someone's theory about it.

With the collapse of Communism and the major question marks being raised, fairly and unfairly, about Marxist interpretations of society, liberation theology may well turn out to have been a relatively short-lived phenomenon. Its real significance lies in having burst open the norms and traditions of much of Christianity and in having asked some weighty questions which still need to be confronted, not so much by academic theology as by the living Church.

However, basic Christian communities and liberation theology are not the only results of turmoil and upheaval in the Third World, especially Latin America. There is another side to the coin – the growth of right-wing Protestant churches. The collapse of the old certainties and structures of the Roman Catholic church following Vatican Two meant that a vacuum was created in certain areas. Marx was after all quite correct when he said that religion is the opiate of the people. He went on to say that it is the sigh of the oppressed – and this is what liberation theology builds upon. But he was also right in emphasizing the dulling dimension of much religion. Many people do not want to be confronted in church with the social, economic and political issues they have to face every day. They come to escape, to experience something else. This need is not met by involved churches. But it is met, *par excellence*, by fundamentalist churches with their clear-cut belief that the Bible is true and foretells what is happening.

To a lesser degree charismatic churches, with their emphasis on the gifts of the Holy Spirit, their enthusiasm and mood of joyfulness, also offer a sanctuary for those afraid of the world outside, or simply tired of the daily grind of living under difficult conditions. Here there can be as strong a sense of community and of belonging, if not a stronger one. In many ways, members of these churches look after each other even better than the basic Christian communities. But the outside world is usually seen as none of their business. They are concerned with the 'path to glory,' with salvation of the individual and with belonging to the elect. In times of turmoil and distress, this kind of Christianity is very popular. Secure within the walls of salvation; seated at the foot of the throne of glory what need is there to care about the worries of the outside world – a world ruled over by Satan and thus naturally at odds with the Christian? The vacuum created by the Roman Catholic shift in orientation has been more than readily filled by such Protestant groups.

The drive to convert people to the narrow, Biblical fundamentalism or charismatic traditions of Protestantism, is fuelled by the traditional hostility of such groups to the Roman Catholic church. They see the Roman Catholics as not only not Christian, but wedded to the forces of the antichrist. The displacement of the Roman Catholics in their own stronghold countries and the conversion of former Catholics to the 'true faith', therefore is all seen as part of a cosmic battle between God and Satan. When you add to this the fact that the Roman Catholic Church, through liberation theology and basic Christian communities, is engaged with Marxists and Communists, then the stage is set for such encounters to be seen as apocalyptic. The rise of radical Catholic theology and action has not just led to the politicization of the people. It has also opened the door to extremist, fundamentalist and right-wing churches to make a considerable mark on the religious life of certain countries. Moreover, it is also moving those countries into a more dependent relationship with the mother of fundamentalism and right-wing churches, the USA.

FAITH AND THE FAITHS

One aspect of the spread of Christianity around the world has been its encounter with other religions. From its earliest days it has had to define itself in relation to other truth claims and religious systems. This has constantly raised a fundamental question. Put very simply, the issue is this: if God has given the fullest revelation through the person of Jesus Christ, what is the point or purpose of other religions? Until recently, most – but not all – Western (Roman Catholic and Protestant) Christians would have said that Christianity would and should replace these other faiths.

The other faiths were interpreted in various ways: as works of the devil to mislead people; as historically useful in that they gave a sense of the spiritual, but now could fade away; as limited pathways to the truth which is Jesus Christ; or as helpful but restricted manifestations of God which are now brought to fulfilment in Jesus Christ. In other words, they were not really relevant to the task of being a Christian in today's world.

There is little doubt that these views were possible because, on the whole, these other faiths were a long way away from the Christian countries which supplied most of the missionaries. Not only were they a long way away, but they were generally in countries which were ruled by the West, and thus they were part of that inferior world which the West was helping towards maturity. The cards, in other words, were heavily stacked against them being taken seriously!

In the last thirty or so years, this has begun to change. The reasons are social as well as theological. The social reasons are migration. As the colonial powers withdrew from their empires, they were followed by migrants from their former colonies, who wanted to share the economic life of the West. In many cases, they were assisted in this migration because the industries of the West, especially in the fifties and early sixties, were short of cheap labour. By the end of the sixties, many cities and towns across western Europe had thriving communities representing a wide range of faiths. Not only that, but teachers from these other faiths, especially Buddhism and Hinduism, were making converts amongst the indigenous populations of western Europe and North America. In the USA, communities of different faiths had been present for much longer, but the official 'melting pot' ideology had militated against their recognition. In the late sixties these communities began to realize that the 'melting pot' idea was not working – at least not for ethnic and religious minorities. In a series of dramatic court cases, such as that of Lau versus the State of California in 1963, the right to be different and to have that difference recognized and even supported by state funds and structures was accepted, changing the 'melting pot' ideology into a pluralist one.

In all this, the old verities of the Christian world seemed to be taking quite a bashing. This was especially true when missionaries from other faiths started making an impact upon the 'Christian' populations of North America and western Europe. In schools, teachers, often Christians, had to try and make sense of their role in nurturing children who came from faiths radically different from their own; of teaching religious education, which had previously been Christian education, in a way that respected the faiths of others; and finally of dealing with the realities of a vibrant, and even at times aggressive, faith other than Christianity, within the local community.

At a practical level, it was in the schools and in the curricula and texts of thinkers and writers of religious education, and to a lesser degree multi-cultural studies, that the first serious reflection on pluralism and Christianity arose. Theology, with a few notable exceptions such as John Hick in the UK and Cantwell Smith in the USA, hardly noticed that there was a problem. Thus, a 'controversial' book of essays on Christ, *The Myth of God Incarnate* could appear in the late seventies without a single essay addressing the significance of Christ in a religiously pluralist society.

On an international basis, the World Council of Churches was only able to appoint a dialogue officer in 1972. Before that it had felt that there was really no point in such a post. The other faiths were, when all was said and done, wrong. When it came, this appointment led to many years of intense discussion and debate, but it marked a watershed, in that the churches accepted that there was something worth discussing with other faiths. For the Roman Catholics, dialogue with other faiths became possible after the Second Vatican Council of the sixties. However, unlike the majority of Protestant churches, the Roman Catholics had some pioneers in this field as far back as the sixteenth and seventeenth centuries, especially amongst Jesuit missionaries like Matteo Ricci in China.

Today, it is probably fair to say that the relationship between Christianity and the other major faiths is something which most

Christians feel is important. Some believe other faiths to be either 'nice but wrong' or 'demonic and therefore dangerous'. But the majority feel that the major faiths should at least work together, even if they disagree, and some would say that all religions are the same, or at least on the same path. For many Christians, Christ has ceased to be the exclusive revelation of God's love and has become a unique revelation of the fullness of God's love. This leaves space for other faiths to be part of the same journey, but not as full a part of Christianity.

Christianity has a major problem with other faiths which arises from its roots in the Greek philosophical world of Plato and the Neoplatonists, a problem shared with many other manifestations of Western thought and society: it cannot accept that diversity is as valid as unity. The origins of this view lie in Plato's desire to find an underlying principle behind the variety and diversity of the Greek gods and beliefs. In seeking this he posited an unchanging, unemotional (unlike the gods of Olympus!) and unaffected One – what he termed Mind. Plato's philosophy sought to reconcile or subsume all under that One, that indivisible unity at the heart of all.

In contrast, much of the Old Testament, and of Hebrew thought, generally points to a more diffuse understanding of God. In some places, the Old Testament is clearly henotheistic – it believes in Yahweh as God, but does not necessarily believe he is the only God. In other places, God is pictured as King of the Gods – as in Psalms 82: 1, 89: 1–10 and 95: 3. In Hebrew thought it is God's dynamism and action which is the focus of attention. In Greek thought, it was the remoteness and absoluteness of God which was most important. The triumph of the remote, Neoplatonic God over the participatory, active God of the Hebrews laid up many problems for Christianity.

This theme, that ultimately the nature of life was One and unchanging, encountered the emotional and emotive God of Israel when Christianity began to spread amongst the Gentiles. Over the first two or three centuries, the struggle to make sense of the two understandings of the divine, the Hebrew and the Greek, led to what was in effect the victory of the Greek model. With the triumph of Christianity as the official state religion, the victory of this model had a social counterpart. For the Roman Empire after Constantine's conversion to Christianity sought to impose orthodoxy as an essential part of its own socio-political unity. What is more, it saw such unity as a divinely necessary condition for the well-being of humanity.

The drive to bring everyone back to an underlying unity and oneness has fuelled Western activities, religious and secular, ever since. It manifests itself in the Church and its mission to convert the world; it is there in the desire of the West to impose its version of democracy on the rest of the world; it was a motivating force in colonialism; it fuelled international Marxism and even the Humanist movement; it is there in the missionary attitudes of Western social concern groups from environmental-ists to peace workers, who believe they have the answer and all would be well if only everyone were like them. It is even there in the impact of this model of One in Islam, which was itself deeply affected by the debates and language used by Orthodox Christianity in the sixth and seventh centuries.

It is quite frankly, such a powerful model that we forget it is only that – a model. Yet it has effectively prevented Christians and others shaped by it from being able to respond creatively to diversity. Diversity – religious, social, economic and even political – is seen as in some way challenging the One and thus as subversive. The reaction of the Belgian colonial officer to the rise of the Kimbanguists is a classic example of the profound sense of unease that diversity poses to the Western mind.

In such a framework, there is no room for diversity on the religious front. But we do not need to be trapped in this model. It is, after all, only one dimension of the Christian understand-ing, drawing not just upon its Greek insights but upon the very different insights of Judaism. As we have seen, it is also possible to understand the core of the Christian message through Celtic imagery and gods and through classical Chinese philosophy or Buddhism. So what does all this mean for the future of Christi-anity, especially in the West?

6

Stories We Must Tell; Stories We Must Drop

As I said in Chapter 1, I grew up on a tough housing estate on the outskirts of Bristol. Being a child of the vicarage, I was naturally brought up as a Christian. Being a Christian on that housing estate was not easy. Few people came to church regularly, though many sought its help and protection when things went wrong, or its blessing and celebration at feast days and family events such as weddings.

I grew up in an atmosphere where the idea of each denomination working away by itself was a luxury we could not afford and did not want. The churches collaborated and the worship sought to reflect the realities of the world as well as to offer a glimpse of another dimension to life. What I remember most powerfully from my childhood is the fellowship we had, both in the worship, but as importantly, in the friendships, the social life and the celebrations of life which the Church enabled us to articulate.

When I first attended a World Council of Churches event, in San Francisco in the early eighties, I joined a group of Christians from around the world. Standing together in a circle around the altar, I looked at the mixed group that we were. There were women in saris and other forms of dress native to their own countries, and men in the habits of religious orders, in Mao suits and in an array of other dress, again drawn from many different cultures. Suddenly I found myself transported. I felt that there was a direct link, a fellowship which drew all these people and the people I had grown up amongst in my home church, into one glorious assembly. For the first time I understood the notion of the communication of saints, of being caught up into the universal and eternal Church. It was a moment of such sweetness and joy that I still feel the excitement as I write.

Such moments are few and far between, but they are food to the soul and body. Much of the time I attend church out of a dogged loyalty and because I find that when I least expect it, God reaches out and touches me. But I am often asked what I believe, and how working every day with different faiths, both here and around the world, affects my faith.

I draw strength from many sources as a Christian involved both in a wide range of secular issues – the environment, economics, education – and in a diverse array of faiths. I believe that Christianity makes more sense of the world than any other system I have encountered. But it is not the Christianity of the first century, nor that of the sixth century, the eleventh century or even the Reformation. It is the Christianity which I see emerging and at times being rediscovered all around me. Here I would like to draw together some of the strands which have appeared in the earlier chapters in order to see what it is that I believe Christianity is and can be, and why it is that I still remain a Christian.

IN THE BEGINNING . . .

I suppose I should start at the beginning: creation. I do believe that there is a purposeful God behind, within and through creation. I find not the slightest difficulty in believing that God has used the tool of evolution to develop creation. I believe that time and place began at a definite time, though how, or even why, I am a little more agnostic about! I believe that God is present in all creation, but is not contained by creation. What I do not believe is that creation has taken place for our sake, nor do I believe that humanity's foolishness and wickedness has led the rest of creation into evil or corruption.

Let me unpackage this a little. God the creator is not some

remote deity who, to use the famous expression, wound up the world like a clock and set it going. The reason God is the creator is not because God is a distant, all-powerful being, but because God is love and love requires a partner. Creation is the natural outcome of the love of God. It is not a perfect world or universe. It is a creation which exists in dynamic relationship with God, for otherwise love would have created a slave. The creation has a life of its own. It has laws and patterns which have derived from God but have developed through the fact of the existence and growth of creation itself.

Let me give an example. Hundreds of thousands of species came and went on this planet long before humanity appeared. Entire species dwelt here for hundreds of millions of years, completely at home in their environment, until that environment underwent vast changes, the conditions altered, and the species, failing to adapt, perished. The trilobite is a classic example. For over 250 million years, it roamed the seas, perfectly adapted to its surroundings. Then, some 150 million years ago, it died out. And we all know about the dinosaurs who dwelt on earth for many millions of years and then passed away. What is the purpose of such species? They have nothing whatsoever to do with humanity; they are not victims of our greed or of 'the fall'. They have simply existed and then passed away. The only answer that makes sense to me, unless you use the chance theory, is that they had meaning and purpose because God loved them and loved all that they were. I believe God suffered when such species passed away, that creation was diminished, but that it continued and evolved to fill the space they left.

OF GOD AND LOVE

God, it seems to me, is both the lover of all creation and the wise parent who knows when to let their young go, even if the cost is death. To hold on in order to prevent events happening is to deny the life of the other. In Hosea 11, there is a touching account of how God is angry and distressed at the behaviour of

Judah and Israel, the two children whom God has taught to walk and to know the world. God seems at one point to be ready to destroy them both because they are going their own way, but holds off saying:

> My heart recoils from it,
> my whole being trembles at the
>   thought.
> I will not give rein to my fierce
>   anger,
> I will not destroy Ephraim again,
> for I am God, not man:
> I am the Holy One in your midst
> and have no wish to destroy.

I believe this is how God relates to all life. God's compassion is beyond reckoning, but likewise God's love recognizes that to hold on to that which is created or to make it do what you want, is to turn love into slavery. This does not mean that God has simply wound up the world and then lets it run its own course, while observing from on high.

I find this hard to articulate, but the writer Helen Waddell once summed it up most powerfully. In her book *Peter Abelard*, she tells of how the great twelfth-century theologian Abelard and his friend Thibault were out walking in the countryside one day when they heard the terrified cry of a trapped rabbit. The friends rush to help it:

The rabbit stopped shrieking when they stooped over it, either from exhaustion or in some last extremity of fear. Thibault held the teeth of the trap apart and Abelard gathered up the little creature in his hands. It lay for a moment breathing quickly, then in some blind recognition of the kindness that had met it at the last, the small head thrust and nestled against his arm, and it died.

It was the last confiding thrust that broke Abelard's heart. He looked down at the little draggled body, his mouth shaking. 'Thibault', he said, 'do you think there is a God at all? Whatever has come to me, I earned it. But what did this one do?'

Thibault nodded.

'I know', he said, 'only – I think God is in it too.'

Abelard looked up sharply.

'In it? Do you mean that it makes him suffer, the way it does us?'

Again Thibault nodded.

'Then why doesn't he stop it?'

'I don't know,' said Thibault. 'Unless — unless it's like the prodigal son. I suppose the father could have kept him at home against his will. But what would have been the use? All this,' he stroked the limp body, 'is because of us. But all the time God suffers. More than we do.'

Abelard looked at him puzzled.

'Thibault, when did you think of all this?'

Thibault's face stiffened. 'It was that night', he said, his voice strangled. 'The things we did to — to poor Guibert . . .' Thibault stopped. 'I could not sleep for nights and nights. And then I saw that God suffered too. And I thought I would like to be a priest.'

'Thibault, do you mean Calvary?'

Thibault shook his head. 'That was only a piece of it — the piece that we saw — in time. Like that.' He pointed to the fallen tree beside them, sawn through the middle. 'That dark ring there, it goes up and down the whole length of the tree. But you only see it where it is cut across. That is what Christ's life was; the bit of God that we saw. And we think God is like that because Christ was like that, kind, and forgiving sins and healing people. We think God is like that for ever, because it happened once, with Christ. But not the pain. Not the agony at the last. We think that stopped.'

Abelard looked down at him . . . He could have knelt before him.

'Then, Thibault,' he said slowly, 'you think that all this,' he looked down at the little quiet body in his arms, 'all the pain of the world, was Christ's cross?'

'God's cross,' said Thibault. 'And it goes on.'

(*Peter Abelard*, by Helen Waddell, Constable and Co., 1933)

That for me is one of the most moving expressions of the relationship between God and creation that I have encountered. Jesus gave us an image of this kind of love, which lets go but never ceases to love. The parable of the prodigal son is about the risks of love and the necessity to let people go. For me God is no distant deity watching the machinations of the world unmoved. Nor is God the just Judge who has judged the world, and especially humanity, and found it wanting. God's creativity is entirely due to love, and that means both the creativity and the pain of creation.

In Job 38–39, God sings a hymn in praise of creation. God is shown revelling in creation and almost gloats over poor Job about all those dimensions which Job has never seen but which God delights in. I think this is a very important insight into creation. For it says that it has meaning and purpose for God, and it is really of very little significance whether humanity ever uses, sees or even knows about the existence of aspects of it.

Sadly our salvation theology has rarely if ever understood this. I think it was H. G. Wells who said that if horses had a religion, their God would look like a horse! That is precisely our problem. We have written an account of the purpose of our existence – the Bible – and have then assumed that this was the only purpose for all creation – a very mighty jump. We have even done this when telling the stories and myths of science. We create a version of evolution which seems to lead, inexorably and inevitably, to us human beings sitting at the top of the tree of evolution. We have been mightily presumptuous.

I do not believe that creation has taken place with us in mind. I do not believe that we are the purpose or end result of creation or evolution. We are but one species amongst many on a small planet circling around a moderately important sun in one amongst a number of galaxies. Our place in creation is very, very small. We happen at this time to have immense power of life and death over millions of our fellow creatures on earth, but that will pass, either because we will destroy most of them and then ourselves, or because we might actually grow up and evolve a working relationship with the rest of creation. The fact is that life will go on either with us or without. We are not all that God requires of existence.

The remarkable thing is that given how insignificant we are, God does love us, as God loves the sparrow or the flower in the field. But we delude ourselves if we think that God created everything in heaven and on earth, over billions of years, just so that we could strut the stage of the world for a remarkably brief time.

Therefore we need to throw away the anthropocentrism –

the 'we are the centre of the universe' mentality – which so afflicts us. Only God is the centre of life. This view was forcefully stated at the historic gathering of all the patriarchs of the Orthodox church in March 1992. For the first time in history, they all met, in Istanbul, to debate issues of major concern to the churches. In their statement issued on 15 March, the feast day of Orthodoxy, they pointed to 'the failure of all anthropocentric ideologies' which have caused people to seek for 'happiness and fullness of life' through science and technology or through 'nearly idolatrous attachments to material values'.

This is a blow to our self-esteem. After all, we have behaved for centuries as if we were the centre of the world and the purpose of its existence. We are not, and this is proving to be a tough bullet to bite. I think the Nestorian documents and the Celtic prayers give us a way of seeing ourselves as part of this bigger and much more significant picture of God's purpose in creation. The emphasis in the Nestorian documents on Christ coming to save all living things, all beings, and the emphasis in the Celtic prayers on our inter-relationship with nature and thus with God, show us how a less anthropocentric Christian understanding could be expressed.

Some Christians fear that this smacks of pantheism. That is not what I am positing. I am not suggesting that nature itself is sacred, but that its purpose and meaning are. In the past, we have allowed ourselves to cast the sacred out of creation and this has left us with a supermarket view of that creation. It is there for us to use, without questioning why it exists and whether it could exist in its own right. This view has to go, for not only is it false to Christianity's claim that God's essence is love, but it is also destroying the planet.

EVIL AND THE EVIL ONE

The question of what makes us behave as we do towards the planet and one another brings us to the issue of evil. I believe that evil exists because of human action, inaction, folly and vice.

As such it is a part of the problem of who and what we are. The idea of the devil is alien to the heart of the Christian message, which states that there is one God only and no other power. Christians who believe in the devil often talk as if he were an equal power, another deity. This contradicts the Christian believe in the 'Three in One', to use the Nestorian phrase. Belief in the devil is a late development in Judaism and I have discussed its rise in my book *Dancing to Armageddon*. Suffice it to say here that if the world, all creation, is an expression of love, then there can be no devil, no force which is there solely to cause evil. The Old Testament only knows of the devil as the prosecuting angel of God – part of the heavenly court. Thus is he pictured in the opening chapters of the Book of Job. Likewise, this is how he is pictured in Jesus' encounter with him in the wilderness. Here the devil tests Jesus' understanding of his own ministry.

The devil as a force of out and out wickedness simply has no place in God's creation, but is a useful invention for us. In having a devil who is the agent of evil, we have been able to shift blame from ourselves on to another force. The perennial cry of children, 'It wasn't me it was him' is what belief in the devil is all about. It stops us growing up and recognizing what we really are. It also leads to the belief that if the devil exists and if he is a force able to combat God, then he has to have a dominion. If heaven is God's province, then the earth must be the devil's. This was taken to the furthest extreme by the gnostics and Manichaeans, who believed that the world was not just the province of the devil, but was actually created by an evil power. While most Christians reject this, the idea of some sort of cosmic battle between the devil and God with poor humanity stuck in between has been a feature of much Christian teaching. This in turn has led to the material world, and as a direct corollary, our earthly bodies, being seen as demonic or at least bad if not actually evil. Augustine carries some blame for this but his original teachings always contained elements which showed another view. Sadly this balance has been often lost by later writers.

If we are not careful, by believing in the powers and

dominions of the devil, we place God as one of two divine forces. We turn this world, created in love, into a sort of no-go area for the creator and we divert away from ourselves the responsibility for our own actions, both good and bad. So the devil has had his time but is not needed any more. For both Christianity and humanity to grow up, we must dismiss him from our stories.

Dropping the Devil, Retelling the Fall

So, if we get rid of the devil, what are we to make of the Garden of Eden and the fall? Surely, some will argue, it was the devil that tempted Adam and Eve to sin. But this is not true. The story as told in Genesis makes no mention of the devil, Satan or indeed any evil force or power. The snake only came to be seen as a symbol of the devil very much later. There is no inherent evil in what is portrayed as happening in the garden. So what is that whole story, or rather what are those stories in Genesis 1 and 2 about?

I believe those stories show us that we are a part of God's creation, but a part which has exercised its freedom in ways which far exceed that of any other species which we know. By elevating ourselves in our own imaginations, we have ceased to understand our place within the wider world and purpose of God. This has led us to alienate ourselves, from God, from the rest of creation, from each other. I have no idea where or when we began to think that we were different, but if there was a fall, then it came when we began to have self-knowledge, and with that self-knowledge, began to elevate ourselves into the centre of meaning.

There was no historical fall, no date when humanity fell from grace. What there is is the story of our constant struggle and fall. As there was never an Adam and Eve in history, there was therefore never the 'original sin' from which we are all morally descended. The classic definition of original sin is that it is the state of sin within which humanity has lived since Adam's original act of rebellion. It is passed on from generation to generation, says the classical Roman Catholic view, through concupiscence and the actual act of sexual intercourse which creates each person. But the whole edifice of original sin and sexuality so beloved by the Roman church is a fiction which is frankly of little use to anyone except as a means of guilt. What the story of Adam and Eve is about is us, each one of us, now, in our own times. The fall is the inability to be what God requires of us and has nothing to do with the physical body or sexuality. We need to discard all that, for it obscures the eternal truth about us which lies at the heart of the vitally important story — but not history — of the Garden of Eden.

I think that Pelagius, with his belief that humanity is inherently good, was on the right lines, though I also believe that having abolished the devil, we now have to take more seriously the evil and folly which arises from within us. No one looking back over the history of this century, with its terrible wars, its genocidal actions, its poverty and the resulting deaths of millions, can believe that human beings are just good or that we are gradually getting better. What this century above most others has shown us is the depths to which we can sink, the power of fear, the abuse of power and the violence which lies within all of us.

At the same time, the potential for good, the ability of people even under the most appalling conditions to survive and to love, bears witness to the good which is within us all. We should banish for ever the idea that we are bad, for that will simply lead us to behave like children in a class who get a name for being difficult and then play up to the image. But we should also treat with considerable caution those who tell us that we are all good and have untapped potential which just needs exploiting. We are not all good. We are a curious mixture, and as with any mixture need to be handled with care.

The argument used by some to redefine the idea of original sin as something we inherit is that we are not in autonomous charge of our lives. What we can and cannot do, the social and economic circumstances of our birth and life, the type of parents, friends and surroundings we have — all these are forces about which we have very little say, but which shape and determine us to a certain degree. But I do not believe that that original sin is what this is about. I think the Nestorians had it right when they said that the actions of those who came before us condition us, both by their good deeds and their bad, but the teaching of Jesus can break us free from this inheritance.

Once we banish the devil and reject unhelpful, even dangerous notions of original sin, we can begin to be more realistic about what our problem is. Our problem is that humanity has developed a sense of self and a desire for control which has taken us out of the normal patterns of evolution. In doing so we have become self-conscious beings who act in ways which are highly contrary and which also have an impact on those around us and those to come. Our capacity for both good and evil lies within us, but is brought to the fore by the expectations and challenges we confront. Graham Greene once said that the prayer of confession in the old 1662 Anglican Prayer Book always sounded to him like an old offender up before the judge once again. In other words, the attitude developed by our expectation of guilt and of sin makes us believe we can do no good. This in its own way reinforces itself and gives us a low expectation of ourselves.

Yet the coming of the Word of God, the child of God in human form in the incarnation of Jesus Christ, should give us the greatest hope. The incarnation is a massive affirmation of being human, as Pelagius rightly saw. It is an affirmation of what we can be, as Athenasius saw when he said that God became human in order that humans could become God.

SIN AND LOVE

So where does sin enter in? It is not the work of the devil, for he does not exist. It is not our essential nature created by original sin, for God created us in love and has affirmed our potential in the incarnation. Sin is the refusal to believe this and the desire to assert ourselves against the rest of life, God and, so often, our fellow human beings. Sin comes from not believing in the security and meaning which God imparts to us as part of creation. It comes when we use our powers of self-knowledge to elevate ourselves at the expense of others. This is why the prophets of Israel railed against those who abused power, who ignored the poor and the helpless or who gave themselves graces and authority in the name of God. These are all betrayals of the godly within us and are abuses of the potential both within us and within those around us.

The converse of this is also true. If we are secure in God and understand our place within God's wider purpose, we can be partners in this purpose, or vehicles of God's grace. It is very interesting to study the early eucharistic liturgies. In the earliest liturgies – from the third to the fifth centuries – there is very little about sin or guilt. The eucharist is the celebration of life and of the promise of life everlasting. While there was always a recognition that we needed to be sorry for the harm and damage we had done, this was a corporate expression and came within the overall theme of rejoicing. Over the centuries, the liturgy became less and less celebratory and more and more doleful, until we arrive at Graham Greene's sense of being an old offender up before the judge. The celebration has been diminished because we have lost sight of the worth of our existence.

When Jesus wanted to illustrate the potential we have for being vehicles of love or for ignoring the need for love in others and thus falling short of our potential, he told the story of the sheep and the goats.

> When the Son of Man comes in his glory, escorted by all the angels, then he will take his seat on the throne of glory. All the nations will be assembled before him and he will separate people one from another as the shepherd separates sheep from goats. He will place the sheep on his right hand and the goats on his left. Then the King will say to those on his right hand, 'Come, you whom my Father has blessed, take for your heritage the kingdom prepared for you since the foundation of the world. For I was hungry and you gave me food; I was thirsty and you gave me drink; I was a stranger and you made me welcome; naked and you clothed me, sick and you visited me, in prison and you came to see me.'

Then the virtuous will say to him in reply, 'Lord, when did we see you hungry and feed you; or thirsty and give you drink? When did we see you a stranger and make you welcome; naked and clothe you; sick or in prison and go to see you?' And the King will answer, 'I tell you solemnly, in so far as you did this to one of the least of these brothers of mine, you did it to me.'

Next he will say to those on his left hand, 'Go away from me, with your curse upon you, to the eternal fire prepared for the devil and his angels. For I was hungry and you never gave me food; I was thirsty and you never gave me anything to drink; I was a stranger and you never made me welcome, naked and you never clothed me, sick and in prison, and you never visited me.'

Then it will be their turn to ask, 'Lord, when did we see you hungry or thirsty, a stranger or naked, sick or in prison, and did not come to your aid?' Then he will answer, 'I tell you solemnly, in so far as you neglected to do this to one of the least of these, you neglected to do it to me.'

(Matthew 25: 31–45.)

This story is of the encounter of love by love. It is a wonderfully affirmative story about our potential to be channels of God's love. It ties in well with the way the Ecumenical Patriarch of Constantinople sees our relationship with the rest of nature.

Just as the priest at the Eucharist offers the fullness of creation and receives it back as the blessing of Grace in the form of the consecrated bread and wine, to share with others, so we must be the channel through which God's grace and deliverance is shared with all creation. The human being is simply yet gloriously the means for the expression of creation in its fullness and the coming of God's deliverance for all creation.

(*Orthodoxy and the Ecological Crisis*, Ecumenical Patriarchate, Fener, 1989, p.8)

The word that is often used to express this idea of our relationship, our loving kinship, with the rest of creation, is 'blessing'. For so long we have sought to be the dominant ones, to rule, to tame nature or, to use Marx's phrase, to 'break nature'. The Orthodox vision takes our central importance, but turns this on its head and asks that we imitate Christ who was the Lord of all yet came to serve all; it asks us not to be the pinnacle of creation, but rather to be a channel of grace and love, in order that we might be a blessing. It calls for the sort of radical dethroning of the human which then perhaps offers a way forward for the rest of creation.

'WHO DO PEOPLE SAY THAT I AM?'

What then is the role of Christ in such a theology? Yet again I find it in the Celtic and Nestorian prayers. It is there in the idea of the soul friend in Celtic prayer and in the vision of the trinity working together as lovers, providers, protectors and guides for the Christian and for all creation. To this I would add the two images that I find most beautiful in the Nestorian texts. The first is that Christ became incarnate to be the scaling ladder and rough-hewn stone steps by which we, the sick and weary, might ascend to the Mountain place of Rest and Joy. This captures for me the sense of Christ as the Way and the Path which lead us to God and to that peace which the world cannot give. The second image is that Christ became flesh and suffered and died and thus made 'the whole world to know that a human life is as precarious as the candle flame'.

In Christ we meet the One who walks with us, carries us, loves us and needs us. We also meet the One who can lead us on our journey through life and beyond, the one who helps us to scale the Mountain of Rest and Joy. This is no remote deity working miracles for us, or plucking us from the grasp of evil forces. This is the One who has walked this way himself and who knows the hardships and the joys of the journey.

In Christ I believe we encounter the potential within us all that God wishes us to draw forth. I believe that in the way Christ was and acted we see the model for ourselves. I believe that in drawing out from us our worst, in that when love came we feared it and sought death for it, Christ holds a mirror to us in which we can see both the good and the bad. But most of all Jesus showed us the cost of love and the precariousness of life.

For me this is beautifully captured in Oscar Wilde's story *The Selfish Giant*.

The Wounds of Love

The story tells of a beautiful garden which belonged to a giant. While he was away visiting friends for many years, the local children found their way into the garden and it was their favourite place to play. The giant returned and was furious to find the children in the garden. He drove them away and built a high wall with notices saying he would prosecute any trespassers. The wall worked. No children entered the garden, but neither did spring or summer. The garden remained in the depths of winter and became a playground for the frost and hail and cold winds.

One day the giant awoke to hear the most beautiful music in the world. It was a linnet singing in the trees, but no bird had entered the forbidden garden for years. Rushing to his window, the giant saw that a hole had been made in the wall and children sat in every tree. Each tree had broken into full blossom, bar one. Right at the end of the garden, one tree was still wrapped in winter and beneath it a tiny boy was trying to reach up to the tree. The tree was bending its branches down, but they could not reach the boy.

The giant realized how selfish and foolish he had been and, running into the garden, he crept up behind the tiny child and gently lifted him into the tree. Immediately the tree burst into flower. The child turned and flung his arms around the neck of the giant and kissed him. The giant thought he would die with happiness.

Taking a great axe, he broke down the wall and told the children that they would always be welcome. They played all day and when the giant came to say goodnight to them he asked where the tiny child was. They replied that they did not know.

Each day the giant welcomed the children into his garden and each day he hoped to meet the child again. But years went by and the child did not return. The giant grew old and weary, but he would sit and watch the children, always hoping that his special friend would come again.

One winter he awoke and looked out at the frozen garden. Then he rubbed his eyes in astonishment. In the farthest corner one tree had burst into blossom. And there, standing beneath it, stood the child whom the giant loved. The giant ran down the stairs and out into the garden full of happiness and joy. But as he came near to the child his face grew red with anger and he said:

'Who hath dared to wound thee?' For on the palms of the child's hands were the prints of two nails and the prints of two nails were on the little feet..

'Who hath dared to wound thee?' cried the Giant; 'tell me that I might take my big sword and slay him.'

'Nay!' answered the child; 'but these are the wounds of love.'

'Who art thou?' said the Giant, and a strange awe fell on him, and he knelt before the little child.

And the child smiled on the Giant, and said to him. 'You let me play once in your garden, today you shall come with me to my garden, which is Paradise.'

And when the children ran in that afternoon, they found the Giant lying dead under the tree, all covered with white blossom.

It is this notion of love that draws me to Christ, the love which knows that to love is costly, but that love without cost is no love at all. It is both the historic Christ that I encounter here, and the cosmic Christ – the Christ who transcends time and place. He does so by being present in all – see Matthew 25 – and by being beyond this world in the sense of being part of the dynamic harmony which the Celtic church saw and experienced so vividly in the trinity and which Oscar Wilde captures in this tale.

Soul Friend and Flickering Candlelight

I find the Celtic idea of Christ as soul friend and the Nestorian view of his life as like a fragile light which we are called to defend and protect to be a very powerful set of images. The fragility of Christ did not cease when he grew from the baby of Bethlehem into the young man of Galilee. His vulnerability is in all pain and suffering in the world. His cross is the acts of cruelty and selfishness which scar the world. His friendship is that he is always with us. There is a story told about a person who dies and meets Christ. Together they look back over the person's life. There, marked on the sands of time, is the track made by this woman as she moved through life. Beside her walk another set of footprints. Christ says, 'You see, I walked beside you through your life.'

But the woman replies, 'Yes Lord, but at the times when life became most difficult and painful, there is only one set of footprints. Where were you then?'

'My friend', replies Jesus, 'there is only one set of footprints because that is when I carried you.'

I think that we need to discard for ever the idea of Christ as a sacrifice made to appease an angry God. This is frankly blasphemy and denies us that relationship with the creator and with the Son which the Celts knew and valued so greatly, the relationship of dwelling within the blessing of the trinity.

What God sought through Christ was to draw humanity back to the light of the truth and, through such truth, to free us to be. It was not in order to load us down with self-pitying guilt. This is often nothing less than a perverse form of self-elevation. By feeling worm-like we demand that God constantly tell us that we are loved, and this is to demand centre stage again. It is the mirror image of the self-righteousness that Christ so forcefully condemned. Self-abnegation and self-abuse in the form of extreme asceticism or shutting out the beauties of the world is anti-Christian. The story of Moling (pp. 83–4) illustrates this. It is also worth recalling the Jewish rabbinical saying, that we shall be judged and condemned for all the pleasures and delights of this world which we could legitimately have enjoyed, but did not!

God in Christ calls us to be fully his, and to know that if we fall short, Christ is there to carry us until we can stand again; that in the weakness and needs of those around us, Christ meets us and asks for recognition.

I believe that the Holy Spirit is the wind of life which moves us forward and sustains us; that as the Nestorians, living in the heat of Central Asia described it, it is the cool wind which refreshes us and it is that spirit which breathes upon us in every friendship and encounter of love.

OUR SPECIES WILL DIE TOO

I also believe that this world will end at some time, but that for us to seek to hasten its demise through warfare or environmental destruction is to play at God. This world will pass away because nothing lasts for ever. Even the trilobites died out after 250 million years. If we think that our species, or even our kind of world, will last for ever, we are deluding ourselves, both in terms of evolution and in terms of religious truth. However, the manner and time of the passing away of our species and of this world is not known to us – thank God. All that we can try to do is ensure that its demise is not hastened or precipitated by acts of human folly and greed. I believe it is very important that we accept that our species will die out at some time. Not because I am a fatalist – far from it – but because it reminds us that humanity is just a part of the process of creation and evolution.

THE GODLY NATURE OF DIVERSITY

But what about other faiths and other truth claims? I am often asked, because I work with so many faiths and cultures, what sense I make of them and of their claims, in relationship to the faith and truth claims that I follow.

I believe that we have to use very different images from the ones we have traditionally used. The West has long had an obsession with trying to make everyone the same. The desire to return to Plato's unmovable, unchanging One, the Monad, the Mind, is a very powerful pull in all spheres of Western life. Be it one faith, one economic system, one political system, one ideology – the West, from Christianity through free trade to Marxism, has tried to mould the world in its own image. This means that we have a deep-seated fear of diversity. In part this has been justified by history. The terrible wars of religion of the sixteenth and seventeenth centuries; the wars of nationalism of the late eighteenth and nineteenth centuries and the ideological wars, hot and cold of this century show that diversity can frequently become division. But possibly this is due to the fact that because we don't know how to deal with diversity, we try to make it fit into one model or framework. This then leads to discontent which in turn leads to division and warfare.

Western Christianity has been profoundly affected by this model, and has passed on its impetus to offsprings of Christianity such as capitalism and Marxism. We have tried to suppress diversity, to the extent that whilst we cannot ignore the division of our faith into Catholic and Protestant, we have for centuries ignored the third part, Orthodoxy. It has also meant that we have hunted heretics, for they encapsulate diversity. But what we find most difficult to understand is why other faiths and cultures exist. Because we have swallowed the Greek demand that truth be One, we cannot imagine truth as being diverse – despite believing in the trinity!

Thus all other truth claims have had to be either denied or absorbed within the wider truth of Christianity. I believe this is not what God is telling us in the diversity that exists. At the beginning of this century, the great student evangelical leader and ecumenist, John Mott called for 'the evangelization of the world in this generation'. That did not happen, nor will it ever happen. If anything, the period since John Mott's call has seen an increase in the strength of other faiths and the rise of various new forms of religion.

So what are we to make of diversity? The clue lies in part, I believe, in looking at God in action. If, as a Christian, I profess a belief in God as creator then surely creation will display something of how God works. I believe that evolution is an expression of the love of God. So let us look at how the basic principle of evolution works. For evolution to continue and for new and more adept species to arise there needs to be a pool of genes from which it can develop. There also needs to be as wide a range of different species and sub-species as possible so that as one becomes obsolete, another can emerge from the background to take over. In other words, to use the catch-phrase of the environmentalists, we need 'biological diversity' if life on earth is to be able to continue in any significant way.

If it is through diversity in biology that God works in evolution, then perhaps we have some basis for believing that he generally works through diversity not through unanimity. I would claim that he actually created and uses diversity in order to express the fullness of love and the different outcomes of love which are his very nature. Once we can begin to see diversity as something God-given, not a terrible mistake arising from a Tower of Babel experience which the Church has been sent to tidy up, then we can begin to relate to the rest of the world's faiths.

But let me make one thing very clear. Simply accepting that diversity is of God does not mean that all aspects of diversity are equally valid or true. In biological diversity, there are species which are dying out because they have not adapted to changing circumstances; species which are just struggling into life; some which will never manage to sustain development; some that are parasitical on other species; some that are just coming into their prime; some that are actually inimical to the vast majority of the rest of life. Diversity does not mean all are equally valuable or right. So it is with the diversity of faiths and cultures. There are aspects of all faiths and cultures which are bad. There are some forms of faith which are destructive and which draw out the evil within people. There are some forms which are dying out and will do so quite naturally, there are others which are arising to new significance, and so forth. In this way I believe Christians can accept the reality of diversity but also retain their critical faculties. Furthermore it provides a critical tool for looking at the relevance of Christianity. I would argue that we carry an immense baggage of mistakes, evil decisions, foolish ideas, obsolete terminology, of anachronistic world views and beliefs which are inimical to spiritual growth. But we also carry the truth. The issue is whether we can find it in the midst of the mass of baggage and whether we can have the courage to discard that which we no longer need.

God the Author

This book is about stories, the many and diverse stories of Christianity. It has involved us in looking at what many of us would see as being the main strand of the story – Western Christianity. It has taken us into other stories, such as the story of the Celtic church or the story of the Nestorians. There are many other stories to tell, at which we have only hinted; the story of the peoples of the 'two-thirds world' who see liberation in Christ, for example, and the feminist stories of Christianity. So it is to story that I want to turn in order to try and fit all this into some sort of pattern.

Imagine that the story of life on earth is exactly that – a story. Imagine that God is the story-teller, who finds, as so many story-tellers do, that the characters take on a life of their own – this is one of the joys and pains of creativity and integrity. So the whole of life – the planets, the cooling of earth, the falling of the first waters, the first cell of life, the trilobites, belemites and dinosaurs, the mammals and the humans – are all books in the same series. Imagine that the story of human life on earth is just one of the books. In such a book, such a novel, a good story-teller will have a variety of plots and sub-plots. It is the interaction between these different stories within the story, within the series, which makes a good novel.

Using this model, we can see that the church has often tried to say that there is just one story – us. The sub-plot is creation, and the main, indeed in some readings the only, characters are the Christians. In this version of the story, Christians have to appear on every page, for without them there is no story.

Now imagine the story as being just one amongst a whole

series, a series which the author obviously intends to go on well beyond this particular volume. Imagine that the story contains a host of characters, stories and sub-stories. Within this, the Christian story is an integral part and has its role in helping bring to fruition or to grief certain other stories or sub-plots. But it is not the only story and nor is it necessary for Christians to appear on each page, or even in each chapter. I would hazard a guess that this would be a much more complex but more interesting novel.

This I believe is what God the novelist is doing. We need the humility to see that we are part of something much bigger, but this does not stop us being both distinctive and even central to the novel. However, as any good novel will show, you do not have to dominate each page of the book in order to be a central character.

I believe we need to celebrate diversity, not fear it. I believe we need to have the humility to see our place within a wider story. I believe we need to learn from the Nestorians and the Celtic Christians how to draw in the stories of others and make them part of our story, with the risk, even the possibility, that our own story will change in the telling and the encounter. I also believe that we need to be critically aware of the failure to love and of the blinding of love by dogma and doctrine which is often nothing more than antique language which once expressed a truth but which has turned, like a prehistoric sea creature, into a hard fossil. Beautiful and tough as these are, we would be fools to mistake them for real life today.

We Christians are wonderfully blessed. We have a multitude of stories of our faith and its meaning to explore. Some have proved to be dead ends; some have been shunted off into the cold; others have never dared to speak out openly before; yet others wait to arise or are struggling to find the words, the images and the opportunities to emerge. Only a fool would look into the bookshop of Christianity and say that they have read all the books on sale. Even more foolish would be the person who says that the shop only contains one story. It is obvious that for many of my contemporaries in the West, the old story of Christianity has ceased to speak with authority or with meaning. Yet in many parts of the world, others are discovering their own story within the faith and are creating new stories of Christianity. The challenge to us in Western Christendom is: what stories can we tell? For many, the Celtic story offers hope – I would count myself as one. But we would be fools to try and inhabit the fifth- to tenth-century world of the Celts just as we would be fools to try and live in the world of first-century Palestine and the Greek-speaking world. All such stories contain insight; do we have the insight to take these and retell them in language and image that means something to us?

THE STORY-TELLERS OF THE GOSPEL

I find more and more that it is in novels and films that the gospel is most powerfully presented. Often, the writers themselves would not describe themselves as Christians, but their use of and reworking of the basic elements of the stories of Christianity speaks more powerfully and more deeply than the Bible itself. Science fiction provides an excellent example of this. Most good science fiction tries to grapple with perennial issues of human nature: of the origin and purpose of life and the consequences of human 'sin'. Writers such as Terry Pratchett with his Disc-world series of novels such as *Mort*, *Small Gods* and his wonderful *Good Omens*, are able to retell the eternal truths of Christianity in a way which makes them both accessible and appropriate to our age. Films such as *Babette's Feast* and *The Mission* also present us with the heart of the Christian message of love and suffering, the rise of pride and greed, foolishness and arrogance as a barrier to the love of God, and the breaking down of that same barrier by that love, often at great cost.

There are other new story-tellers of Christianity too. The work of many Christian environmentalists, who retell the story of the Garden of Eden, of the creation of humanity and the rest of creation, is forging new understandings of both the vital need for a creation story and the necessity that this story be wider in its implications than has traditionally been the case.

The writings, liturgies and prayers of feminist Christians or of Christians affected by the feminist movement, also shows new story-telling. Perhaps this new telling is one of the most exciting, for it has taught us that the terms 'Father' and 'Son' need to be expanded to tell of a quality of relationship rather than to point to a gender! The liberation from stereotype and masculinity which the feminist movement offers to Christian story-telling is of immense significance. We can begin to abandon the Big Daddy model with all its negative and often aggressive and violent overtones, such as substitutionary atonement, and start to tell of the creator as a life-giving force who not only decrees that life shall come forth, but whose labour pains are part of the process of creation.

New stories are also emerging from the encounter between Christianity and other faiths. In Chapter 5 we saw the way Professor Chung Hyun-kyung of South Korea retold the story of the Holy Spirit through the dramas, tales, personalities and history of her own people and of oppressed peoples throughout history. In the very varied bag of materials which are emerging from cross-cultural interaction and which are sometimes unhelpfully lumped together under the term 'New Age' we can see some remarkable new tellings of the stories of Christianity in ways which often shock or disconcert more traditional Christians.

In responding to these varied and various new tellings of the stories of Christianity, in encountering Christ in such strange garb or in such unusual company, we need to be careful that we do not become like the goats in the story from Matthew 25 told on p. 175. Many within the churches are in danger of failing to see and meet Christ in these new movements, stories and struggles. They say, 'We do not see Christ there', and I fear they will appear as foolish as those who did not recognize Christ in the hungry and imprisoned.

But as ever we also need to keep a critical eye open. Just as diversity means that there is both good and bad within such a range, so the telling of stories always means that some are more helpful than others. This is why we need to reject stories which have crept into Christianity, such as those which picture this world as the domain of an evil force, those which depict God as an unforgiving judge or father, and those which present humanity as inherently evil. These stories may once have been useful, but they are now damaging. Likewise, there will appear stories which are also dangerous: stories which tell us we are perfectible when experience tells us otherwise, stories which claim to have the answer and thus try to stop us making our own journeys, and stories which present us with simplistic dichotomies when we know that such simplicity only comes at the expense of the variety and diversity of life.

I have great faith in the ability of the Christian stories to continue to guide, inspire and teach us. I have this faith because of the many different ways these stories have been told in the past and are being told today.

THE STORY AT RISK

As a Christian, struggling to discern the stories through which Christ is speaking and the Holy Spirit is moving today, I cannot set out for you what the future stories will look like. I have tried to give hints of what I see as being both the core truths around which these stories will naturally form, and to indicate some of the issues which are forcing or enabling a retelling to take place. The excitement of being a Christian story-teller is that often these new stories of Christ arise in contexts where we do not expect them to occur, come from people and groups we did not intend listening to, and confront us in places and ways of which we never dreamed. In my own journey, these encounters have taken place on the housing estate where I grew up; in Buddhist temples in Japan; at a gathering of the heads of different environmental groups from around the world; at the cinema; in popular literature; on rubbish-strewn beaches; in the quiet words of a Russian bishop; at the end of good parties; at communion services; in Hindu temples in India and in Sikh gurdwaras in Manchester. For me, the journey through life is like a vast *Canterbury Tales*. Rooted in the fundamental belief that God is love and guided by the revelation of God's love in Jesus Christ, I find God's stories confront me almost daily. The passion of Christ is happening daily — to people and to the planet. Every day brings crucifixion but also resurrection. Each day brings an encounter with the divine breaking through in the ordinary — incarnation in all I see.

Let me give one example of how I see the story of Christ being retold today in a stark and disturbing way — a way which brings home the truth of the precariousness of life, which the Nestorians spoke of as being the insight given by Christ's passion.

To understand what we are doing to the planet we do not need yet more figures and facts, important though they are. We need a way of interpreting these figures and facts, and of making some sense out of them. For me the events of Holy Week offer just such a framework for understanding. For in what we did to Christ, we can see what we are doing to creation.

On Palm Sunday, Jesus rode into Jerusalem and was greeted by the crowds, and even by the authorities. They cheered him and promised to follow him. Likewise, around the world people and governments have proclaimed ever louder and louder their 'concern', their 'affection' and their intention to work for the well-being of creation.

But Palm Sunday leads through Holy Week to the same crowds and leaders betraying Jesus and calling for his death. On Holy Monday, Christ entered the temple and drove out the moneylenders and those dealing in what should have been holy things. As soon as you take the environmental crisis seriously you realize that unjust economics and the possession of most of the world's goods and wealth by a tiny minority is one of the major reasons for the environmental crisis. Any engagement with creation's well-being means you have to tackle material-ism, modern consumer economics and the power of money over everyone's lives. We need to cleanse our temples.

On Holy Tuesday we encounter the religious leaders seeking to catch Jesus out with trick questions about authority and power. Again, look at what happens when the plight of the earth begins to impinge upon the cosy worlds of religion. My own church, the Church of England, currently has the worst track record of any of the major international denominations in terms of practical action on ecology at leadership level. It is too caught up with the debate about women priests and with picking its way through its commitment to a decade of evangelism – whatever that might mean. The idea that the good news of the gospel might be about the planet, seems to have escaped most of our leadership. So expect no help from those whom one might have supposed would support either the Messiah or the planet. The passion of Christ shows that they fail at the crucial moment.

Holy Wednesday, in the official church calendar, is when we recall the Last Supper. Here we see the fellowship of the friends of Jesus and of Jesus himself. Here are a small group of men and women who are surrounded by hostile forces, who do not fully understand what is happening, but who remain together through fellowship: the solidarity of the small cell, the tight-knit group who continue even when things get rough. But Holy Wednesday also reminds us of the betrayal which can come from those within a small group. It reminds us of the fragility of such a group, yet, in the institution of the communion, we also see how such a fellowship can begin to turn the world upside down, taking defeat and turning it into victory.

Holy Thursday is the betrayal and the trial. Now the knives are out. The conflicting understandings of what Jesus has come to do lead Judas Iscariot to push him into direct confrontation. But Jesus does not then call upon the angels to destroy the soldiers. Instead he gives himself up, a victim to human fear of love. He prepares to go forward to bear the wounds of love. Perhaps the earth has reached this stage. Despite all the fine words, the grand intentions and the mounds of papers, we have brought the creation to the edge of crucifixion. The passion of Christ shows that we did it once before. What is to stop us doing it again unless we listen to this story and see how Christ shows that life is as precarious as a candle flame.

Good Friday brings the crucifixion, the day when we took love and hung it on the cross to die. If this does not shock us today then we need to see, not the all too well-known figure of Jesus upon the cross, but creation, or perhaps even a particular species. For the crucifixion is not just a historical event. It continues to happen every day of the year. Only now, we seem close to bringing much of God's creation, God's expression of love, to an end – and a brutal and mocking end at that. It is when we see the crucifixion in these terms, as something which we are doing now, not something others did back in history, that we hear clearly what God wants to say through the death of Christ. Can we hear, or do our fears, greed, comfortable lifestyles and at times ignorance, blind and deafen us?

Then we come to the resurrection. We know that the passion of the historical Christ has a 'happy ending' and this at times allows us to forget the horror and tragedy of the events of Holy Week. For if we transfer this model to what is happening to so many species and eco-systems, can we be sure of their resurrection? I think not. It is this which should alert us to the road down which we are currently travelling, for it is a road which we have travelled once before, 2000 years ago. Can we hear the cry of Jesus, 'My God, my God, why have you forsaken me', and be sure that such a cry is not going up from all creation? Can we see in those who killed Jesus through fear or indifference ourselves as we marginalize concern for the planet to Sunday supplements and recycling schemes? My contention as a Christian story-teller is that we need to see again the traumas of Holy Week, for they are going on all around us, and I fear we stand on the brink of the events of Good Friday, but without the assurance of the resurrection.

Christ came to bring life and to show both fragility of love and its powers of survival. Can we realize now what this incarnation has to tell us about the stories we are acting out? I hope and pray we can.

MAKING SENSE

As I said at the beginning, I remain happy to call myself a Christian because I still find the faith makes more sense of the world and of myself than any other that I have encountered. I remain deeply frustrated by the way those in authority in my faith frequently tell the stories of Christianity and I am often disturbed by the legacy of certain tellings of the stories. I see more people outside the formal structures of the faith telling anew and often more faithfully the stories of the faith. This is why I have no fears for the continuation of the core truths of Christianity concerning God, life, ourselves and the purpose of our being. The Holy Spirit moves across the face of the world and speaks through those who are willing to be open to its truths. I hope and pray that the churches and Christians will awaken more fully to their ability and right to retell the stories of the faith in a new way. Perhaps I can best conclude this chapter by writing a Celtic prayer of my own.

> I pray to the Three,
> The Author, the Word Incarnate and the Wandering
> Story-teller;
> To the Three,
> The Creator, Created Creator and Creating Creator;
> To the Three,
> Lover, Beloved and Loving,
> That the Church might learn to sing the Lord's Song
>   anew.
> Yet I know,
> That the Three in One
> Will always speak, live and move
> across our world and beyond,
> And I know,
> That if the Church cannot sing the Lord's Song,
> Then the Spirit of the Three will seek others,
> Through whom the Three can speak,
> move,
> and manifest their love.

7

Telling the Stories Anew in Praise and Meditation

Most of this book has been story and discussion. Yet the Christian faith is as much about silence and prayer as it is about action and discussion. Through worship, Christians are encountered by the stories of their faith and the drama of the passion of Christ and the love of God. I want to end this book by simply offering a liturgy of liturgies. In the following pages I have tried to explore the stories of the faith through worship. The following material was written by me for various special liturgies, events and places. I am grateful to the BBC, to the Deans and Chapters of Winchester, Coventry, Canterbury and Washington DC cathedrals; to the Papal Basilica of St Francis, Assisi, Italy and to Michael and Yoshika Shackleton for permission to print material first written for them. I am also grateful to Moyra Caldecott for permission to reprint her dramatic retelling of the creation story. Finally, my thanks to the World Wide Fund for Nature UK and International for their permission to reprint material first written for them. I hope you may find it of use for your own devotions or for use in congregations or communities. It is offered copyright-free, so please feel free to use it, but be so kind as to say where it came from!

MORNING PRAYER

In the beginning was – what?

The Big Bang?

I think not.

For before that there was Quiet,

And there God was.

Reading: I Kings 19: 9–13.

Silent Reflection

'In the beginning was the Word, and the Word was with God, and the Word was God.' (St. John's Gospel 1: 1.)

Outside time the consciousness of God exists.
In that Consciousness
is a thought
of such intensity that within it
all and everything
conceivable and inconceivable
imaginable and unimaginable
possible and impossible
is contained.
That thought is uttered
and from the vibrations of that sound,
from the resonance of that Word,
from what the scientists call
'The Big Bang'.
the multitudinous forms of being are spreading
in ever increasing circles.
The vast universe of whirling forms take shape.
World after world swings through space,
each to each held
by an inner and invisible force,
the whole
a balance of attraction and repulsion.

Within these worlds
light and dark interact.

Aeons pass.

Liquid fire cools to rock,
scaling steam to rain.
More than a thousand million years pass.
More than a thousand million times
the burning orb of the sun rises and sets
over the desolate landscapes of our earth –
its powerful cosmic rays ever active, ever potent.

Cautiously, the first life-forms emerge –
infinitesimal cells divide, join up with others,
subdivide, rejoin.
The liquid oceans seethe with life.
Beings with or without calcareous shells
live and die by their billions
trilobites
graptolites
brachiopods
drifting through the waters for 300 million years
to lie at last on the ancient sea bed,
their minute bodies
forming the fossiliferous rock
we walk so casually upon today,
while the shell of the ammonite
that pumped through the primeval ocean
so vigorously in search of food
has been replaced molecule by molecule by crystal
and lies now, bejewelled in our museums, curled, whorled and
    spiralled.

Some life-forms collect in rock pools,
breathe air,
grow and change.
The first fish struggle on to land
exchanging fins for limbs.
Corals and sponges build their sturdy tenements
and learn communal living in the oceans.

On land, cold-blooded reptiles sun themselves singly
upon the rocks,
mosses and horsetail plants as tall as forest trees
flourish in the marshlands.
Three hundred and fifty million years ago
the coal beds formed as these marshland forests died.
Another 200 million years
and the dinosaurs tread hot sand
leaving their giant footsteps, fossilized.
Where have they gone, these ancient, fearsome beasts?
They with the tiny ammonites and belemnites are now extinct,
Do we still carry them in our blood?

Time moves on.
Small warm-blooded mammals take their place
among the cycads, ginkgoes, ferns and conifers.
Birds sing
and the first flowering plants put out their finery.
Another sixty million years go by
and we rise to our feet,
lift our eyes to the firmament
and begin to name names
and recognize our God.
Still with us
is the impetus of the Word.

Our being is the expression of God's thought.
We contain the love of God and God contains us
and as we unfold on earth
through shell-creature,
fish-form,
reptile,
bird
and mammal –
through icthyosaurs
plesiosaurs
dinosaurs
and ape –
we are learning
step by step
what that containment means.

The circles are still widening –
still evolving the mighty concept –
the magnificent Idea.
Six days,
Seven . . .
a million years,
a thousand million . . .
the count is nothing,
the Being – all.
Praise be to our great God
and the Word that resonates
in our hearts still.
May we not separate ourselves in arrogance
from the Great Work
for we know the sound of the Word
but not its full meaning.

THE THANKSGIVING

Psalm 148.

The psalm of St Columba (see pp. 80–1)

Using the pattern of St Columba's psalm, tell of those things in your own life for which you wish to give thanks. For example, for me the following are a few of the things I wish to give thanks for.

Delightful I think it to be at home, writing in my quiet study, gazing upon my garden, awaiting the children home from school.

That I might hear their voices and know they are well, or being distressed, be on hand for them.

That I might cycle through the streets and enjoy both the rain and the sunshine.

That friends may call to see us and meals be shared, stories told.

That when I travel, I learn from those I meet.

That at times of rest, on flights or in the train, I might think on all I do and do not do and seek the forgiveness of Christ for all that is unworthy in all that I do.

That at the last, I may recall for whom all that I do and am is intended and recalling, that I might sit a while at the feet of love.

THE PASSION

'Then, Thibault,' he said slowly, 'you think that all this,' he looked down at the little quiet body in his arms, 'all the pain of the world, was Christ's cross?'

'God's cross,' said Thibault, 'And it goes on.'

THE PROCESSIONS OF LIFE

Listen to me Jacob,
Israel whom I have called:
I am the first
and I am the last.
My hand laid the foundations of the earth
and my right hand spread the heavens.
When I call to them
they all come forth together.
(Isaiah 48: 12–13)

Listen now. Be still and hear.
For creation takes up the Maker's call.
All creation draws near to God,
seeks refuge from the tightening grip of winter,
the winter our destruction has wrought;
seeks light and warmth to revive that which we have
    darkened
and chilled by our abuse of God's creation.

Listen to the voices of creation.

THE AIR

Lord, I the air come.
Breath of life,
Wind that moves over the face of the deep
Bearing rain,
I come.

Now the breath of life
blows death.
As I pass over the land
the broken soil follows me;
a billowing shroud of dust.

When the rain falls,
forests and lakes die.

I come, my Lord.
But what have your people made of me
but a shadow,
a dark, acidic shadow
of my God-given glory.
Breathe on your people, breath of God.

THE WATERS

We the waters come, O Lord,
flowing to meet you
as we have flowed through time,
sustaining the life of all creation.

We come, O Lord,
from our rivers and lakes
our seas and oceans.

We come, O Lord, with our dead
borne upon our waves.
Our living
struggle against creeping filth
and our mighty creatures
flee before the fury
of your people.

Can we ever recapture
the purity of your will
in the brightness of our waters?
Stir up your people, O Lord,
to let the waters flow
with life everlasting.

THE LAND

Mountain and valley,
hill and plain,
we the land turn to you our Lord,
ground of our ground.

Upon us you set your world,
from us called forth life in many forms.

In our richness
you set the forests.
On our fields
you sowed the seed
of life.

Gone are the forests,
worn is the eath.
Silent in their graves
lie the riches
of your creation.

Gouged out are the mountains,
gone are the curves
of the valley.
We who would bear your creation,
seek re-creation.
Plant in your people a love and respect for your land.

THE CREATURES

From water,
air
and land
we the creatures came forth
at your command.

From dust you raised us
and in us
planted your life.

Through the ways
of time
you brought us
to be.

Now we come
called forth again.
Yet many
can no longer come.
Gone,
gone forever.

And we, we who come.
Can we know our children's
children
will know this world?

So much has gone.
What remains
is so frail.
Free your people
from their ignorance
and selfishness.

HUMANITY

We, your people come.
We who crucify this world,
stripping bare its soil,
crowning it with a wreath of broken trees.
Its air breathes painfully,
its waters weep for the folly that poisons them,
its creatures bleed.
We have eaten and drunk of life's body.

Heirs of all,
we have sold our world.
Thirty pieces of silver is our price.
Loudly declaring our love,
we have denied our Lord.

We are Judas,
we are Peter.
We are the cross of all creation.

FORGIVENESS AND RESURRECTION

We have all fallen short of the glory of God,
Yet we are all children of God.
In silence, let us offer ourselves to God,
who alone knows our strengths and our weaknesses.
Let us ask for forgiveness from those we have hurt;
forgive those who have wounded us,
and learn to forgive ourselves.

Christ died to make known to the whole world that a human life is as precarious as the flame on a candle.

THE INTERCESSIONS

In the eucharist, the thanksgiving, the church offers to God the world and its concerns in prayers of intercession. Often these tend to be prayers which deal with the disasters — earthquakes, wars, famines, unemployment, homelessness, disease and death. These should really be balanced by recalling that which is good in the world — health care, education, successful harvests, peace initiatives, reunions of families, births and marriages, birthdays and celebrations. I leave to you what issue you wish to bring to God, aware of how Christ showed us through his death that life is precarious, like the flame on a candle.

THE COMMUNION

The fellowship offered in Christ is a gift. No one earns it; no one is more worthy of it than any other. Christ's invitation is a simple one:

Come to me all you who labour and are overburdened, and I will give you rest. Carry my yoke and learn from me, for I am gentle and humble in heart, and you will find rest for your souls.

(Matthew 11: 28)

Christ is present at every meal of friendship or of fellowship. The communion should be like a meal, not formalized and deadened, with the bread no more than cardboard and the wine a mere hint.

> I should like to have a great ale-feast for the King of Kings;
> I should like the Heavenly Host to be drinking it for all eternity.
>
> I should like to have the fruits of Faith, of pure devotion;
> I should like to have the seats of Repentance in my house.
>
> I should like to have the people of Heaven in my own dwelling;
> I should like the tubs of long-suffering to be at their service.
>
> I should like to have the vessels of Charity to dispense;
> I should like to have the pitchers of Mercy for their company.
>
> I should like there to be Hospitality for their sake;
> I should like Jesus to be here always.
>
> I should like to have the Three Marys of glorious renown;
> I should like to have the Heavenly host from every side.
>
> I should like to be a tenant of the Lord;
> he to whom He gives a good blessing has done well in suffering
> distress.
>
> (Irish Celtic prayer, tenth or eleventh century. Based on the translation in *A Celtic Miscellany*, by Kenneth Hurlstone Jackson, Penguin, 1951, pp. 284–5.)

Now as they were eating, Jesus took some bread, and when he had said the blessing he broke and gave it to the disciples. 'Take and eat,' he said 'this is my body.' Then he took the cup and when he had given thanks he gave it to them. 'Drink all of you from this,' he said, 'for this is my blood, the blood of the covenant, which is poured out for many for the forgiveness of sins.'

(Matthew 26: 26–28).

Let every meal be the eucharist, every food and drink part of the love of God. Through the offering of bread and wine let us recall what Christ has come to do in us and our world.

THE WAY

The Unique Lord, the Messiah said, 'Truly, truly I say unto you, my teachings can be compared to the Precious Mountain. Its jade forests and pearl fruits, translucent and shining, sweet tasting and beautifully perfumed, can cure a person of hunger and thirst and heal all ills.

There was a sick man who heard of this mountain. Day and night he longed to reach this mountain and the thought never left him.

But sadly, the way was far and the mountain very high and steep. The sick man was also a hunchback and was too feeble to climb such a mountain. In vain did he try to fulfil his dream. He simply could not undertake it. But he had a near relative who was both wise and sincere. This man set up scaling ladders and had steps cut into the mountain and with others he pushed and pulled the sick man up the mountain until he reached the summit. Immediately the sick man's illness was cured.

Know this, Simon Peter, that the people coming to this mountain of true teachings were for a long time confused and in misery because they were burdened by their worldly passions. They had heard of the truth and knew it could lead them to the Way of Rest and Joy – to the Mountain of Rest and Joy. They tried to reach the mountain and to scale it, but in vain, for love and faith had almost died within them.

Thereupon, the Almighty Lord made himself known. He came as the near relative of the people and taught them with such skill and sincerity that they understood that he was both the scaling ladder and the stone steps by means of which they could understand the True Way and rid themselves of their burdens of confusion for ever.

(From the Nestorian *Chih-hsuan-an-lo Sutra*).

MISSION

Life on earth is threatened today by humanity's actions. Just as Christ has reconciled us to God in love, so we need to be reconciled one with another and with all life.

In the story of Noah as told in Genesis, there is a covenant. When God brought Noah safely to dry land, he promised never to destroy life in such a way again. As the Bible says, God made his covenant 'with every living creature of every kind that is found on earth.' The rainbow was given to be a perpetual reminder of that covenant.

Now we need a new covenant. God's promise we do not doubt, for God is the parent of all life, mother, father and lover of all that exists. It is ourselves, humanity, that we cannot trust. We hold the power of life and death over so much of our planet and for so many of our own kind. We have already swept away countless 'living creatures of every kind that are found on the earth'.

In common with millions of other people, from many different faiths, we invite you to make a new covenant. We must now undertake not to wantonly destroy any living creature or damage life on earth to the point of extinction. This covenant is between us and our neighbour, and between humanity and the rest of creation. We invite all people of good will, whatever your faith or belief might be, to join us in the Rainbow Covenant.

Brothers and sisters in creation, we covenant this day with you and
    with all creation yet to be;

With every living creature and all that contains and sustains you.

With all that is on earth and with the earth itself;

With all that lives in the waters and with the waters themselves;

With all that flies in the skies and with the sky itself.

We establish this covenant that all our powers will be used to prevent your destruction.

We confess that it is our own kind who put you at risk of death.

We ask for your trust
and as a symbol of our intention
we mark our covenant with you by the rainbow.

This is the sign of the covenant between ourselves and every living thing that is found on the earth.

EVENING PRAYER

Reading: Luke 22: 39–46.

Christ came to show us that human life is as precarious as the flame on a candle.

As darkness falls upon us and our world, may we prove worthy of the trust and love of God. Let not the sun go down on our anger, nor the sun rise upon our wickedness. In our coming in and our going out, may God bless us and may we make each act of ours praiseworthy to the triune majesty.

As darkness falls, let us bring before the Lover all that mars love and all that scars love and all that denies love. In silence let us offer to the Lover all who are hurt, damaged, ill, alone or afraid.

To the Lover let us bring all for whom today has been joyful, all who have celebrated today, all new births and gentle deaths. In silence let us offer to the Lover, life in its fullness.

MEDITATION

Lord of all hopefulness, Lord of all joy,
whose trust, ever childlike, no cares could destroy,
Be there at our waking, and give us, we pray,
your bliss in our hearts, Lord, at the break of the day.

Lord of all eagerness, Lord of all faith,
whose strong hands were skilled at the plane and the lathe,
Be there at our labours, and give us, we pray,
your strength in our hearts, Lord, at the noon of the day.

Lord of all kindliness, Lord of all grace,
your hands swift to welcome, your arms to embrace,
Be there at our homing, and give us, we pray,
your love in our hearts, Lord, at the eve of the day.

Lord of all gentleness, Lord of all calm,
whose voice is contentment, whose presence is balm,
Be there at our sleeping, and give us, we pray,
your peace in our hearts, Lord, at the end of the day

(Jan Struther 1901–53)

THE PEACE

The peace of God, the peace of humanity,
The peace of Columba kindly,
Mary mild, the loving
Christ, king of tenderness,
The peace of Christ, king of tenderness.

Be upon every window, upon every door,
Upon each hole that lets in light,
Upon the four corners of my house,
Upon the four corners of my bed,
Upon the four corners of my bed.

Upon each thing my eye takes in,
Upon each thing my mouth takes in,
Upon my body that is of earth,
And upon my soul that comes from on high,
Upon my body that is of earth,
And upon my soul that comes from on high.

Further Reading

GENERAL CHURCH HISTORY

Augustine, *City of God*, Penguin Classics, 1972.

Augustine, *Confessions*.

Cohn, Norman, *The Pursuit of the Millennium* Paladin, 1970.

Herrin, Judith *The Formation of Christendom*, Fontana Press, 1989.

Lambert, Malcolm, *Medieval Heresy*, Blackwells, 1992.

Markus, Robert *The End of Ancient Christianity*, 1990.

Pagels, Elaine, *The Gnostic Gospels*, Penguin, 1990.

Rees, B.R., *Pelagius, a reluctant heretic*, Boydell Press, 1988.

Runciman, Steven, *A history of the Crusades*, (three vols.-Vol.1 in particular), Penguin, 1978.

CHRISTIANITY AND CONTEMPORARY CHANGE

Daly, Mary, *Gyn/Ecology*, Womens Press, 1979.

Frye, Northrop, *The Great Code – The Bible and Literature*, Ark, 1983.

Garrison, Jim, *The Darkness of God: Theology after Hiroshima*, SCM, 1982.

Hampson, Daphne, *Theology and Feminism*, Blackwells, 1990.

Loades, Ann (editor) *Feminist Theology – A Reader*, SPCK, 1990.

Miranda, Jose, *Marx and the Bible*, Orbis, 1974.

Needham, Joseph, *Within the Four Seas*, Allen & Unwin, 1969.

Palmer, Martin, *What should we teach?*, WCC, 1991.

Smith, Wilfred Cantwell, *The Meaning and End of a Religion*, SPCK, 1978.

CELTIC CHRISTIANITY

Allchin, A.M. & de Waal, Esther, *Threshold of Light*, DLT, 1986.
Bede, *A History of the English Church and People*, Penguin, 1955.
Bede et al, *The Age of Bede*, Penguin, 1965.
Jackson, Kenneth Hurlstone, *A Celtic Miscellany*, Penguin, 1971.
Thomas, Charles, *Britain and Ireland in Early Christian Times*, Thames & Hudson, 1971.
Toulson, Shirley, *The Celtic Alternative*, Rider, 1987.
de Waal, Esther, *A World made Whole*, Fount, 1991.
de Weyer, Robert van, *Celtic Fire*, DLT, 1990.

NESTORIANS AND CHINA

Badger, Percy George, *The Nestorians and their Rituals*, Vols. 1 and 2, DARF Publishers, 1987.
Budge, E.A. Wallis, *The Monks of Kublai Khan*, Religious Tract Society, 1928.
Ch'en, Kenneth, *Buddhism in China*, Princeton University Press, 1964.
Grousset, Rene, *The Empire of the Steppes — a History of Central Asia*, Rutgers University Press, 1970.
Moule, A.C., *Christians in China before the year 1550*, Octagon Books, 1977.
Palmer, Martin, *The Elements of Taoism*, Element, 1991.
Saeki, P.Y., *The Nestorian Monument in China*, SPCK, 1916.
Saeki, P.Y., *Nestorian Documents and Relics in China*, SPCK, 1937.

Index